HOW to LIVE on WHEAT

Third Edition

From Grain to Table

The Complete Guide to Selecting, Storing, Preparing and Cooking Wheat and other Grains.

Storage
Grinding
Sprouting
Food Combination
Bread Making
Gluten Meat Substitute
Improvised Bread Making
Cast Iron Cookery
Biscuits

Essene Bread
Pan Bread
Sourdough
Baking
Sprouts
Pasta
Dumplings
Salads
Pancakes

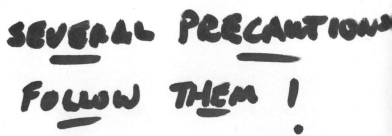

SEVERAL PRECAUTIONS
FOLLOW THEM !

By John Hill

HOW to LIVE on WHEAT

Third Edition

ISBN-13: 978-1-884979-12-5
ISBN-10: 1-884979-12-2

Library of Congress Control No.: 2010918024

BISAC Subject Headings:

CKB098000	**COOKING** / Specific Ingredients / Rice & Grains
CKB007000	**COOKING** / Methods / Quick & Easy
NAT023000	**NATURE** / Natural Disasters
CKB059000	**COOKING** / Specific Ingredients / Natural Foods

Any comments, suggestions or inquiries should be addressed to:

Clear Springs Press, LLC

http://www.clspress.com/contact.html

DISCLAIMER: Safe and effective food storage requires attention to detail and proper equipment and ingredients. There are also variables that include but are not limited to; storage temperature, initial food quality, storage moisture content, storage containers, and the use of storage adjuncts like desiccants and oxygen absorbers. The author has no control over these variables. The author makes no warranties and assumes no responsibility for errors or omissions in the text, or damages resulting from the use or misuse of information contained herein.

Table of Contents

Wheat, Rye, Triticale, Barley, Oats, Buckwheat, Rice, Corn, Millet, Amaranth, Quinoa, legumes, Black Bean, Black Eyed Pea, Kidney Beans, Lentils, Lima Beans, Peanuts, Pinto Beans, Soybeans, White Beans, Peas, Fava Beans, Sweet Lupine

Anti-Nutrients, Anti-Nutrients in Legumes, Phytates, Flavonoids, Food Allergies, Testing for Food Allergies, The Freshness Factor, Checking for Rancidity in Grains and Flour, The Effects of Grinding, Refining and Adulteration, Aflatoxins, Enhancing Wheat Based Nutrition, Adding Legumes to Increase Protein Utilization, Food Combination, Increasing Vitamin Content by Sprouting

Do you want your Food Dead or Alive?, Shelf Life of Grains and Legumes, For Dead Food (Non-Sproutable Grains and Seeds), For Live Food (Sproutable Grains and Seeds), Germination Testing, Storage Containers, Oxygen Absorbers, Desiccants, Moisture Content in Wheat, Measuring Moisture Content in Grain, Selecting and Storing Wheat, Selecting and Storing Other Grains, Protecting Stored Wheat from Insects, Protein Content in Wheat,

Sprouting Wheat, Sprouting Other Grains, Other Sprouting Seeds, Making Wheat Grass, Grinding Sprouted Wheat, Legume Sprouts, Sprouting Legumes, Essene Bread, Making Essene Bread, Sprouted Wheat Bread, Sprouted Wheat Sourdough Bread, Sprouted Wheat Biscuits, Wheat Sprout Pancakes, Stir Fried Sprouts, Hash Browned Potatoes & Sprouts, Mushrooms & Sprouts, Kale, Greens, & Sprouts, Sprout Burgers, Wheat Sprout Salads, Creamed Sprouts, Hot Cooked Sprout Cereal, Sprout Cereals, Sprout Fish Chowder, Important Point

Foreword

Storing food for the security of one's self and one's family is a practice whose merit and wisdom is self evident. The extended aspect is to use this practice as a means of improving one's nutrition and reducing the grocery bill. The challenge is that the practice and protocols of using stored grains and legumes in the daily diet is not the norm for our culture. At first glance, that appears to be an additional task or burden. That is more perception than reality.

The nutritional and economic merits of using freshly ground flour daily are real, not just a philosophy. To use whole grains, one needs to set up a few tools and learn a few new techniques. The tools are a grinder, a sprouting setup, a meat grinder for processing sprouts, a sourdough culture, and a tempeh culture.

One objective is to avoid wasting money by buying storage food and letting it sit on the shelf until it is expired and having to throw it out. Eat what you store and store what you eat is the idea.

The recipes contained in this book are very basic. They are tested and will produce good results, but they should be considered "guidelines" rather than exact formulas. It is important to develop the habit of experimenting, adapting and improvising. That is how all great recipes begin. That is also how you compensate for variables. Your fresh ground flour will not behave the same way as standardized products off of the supermarket shelf. You will also have a flavor advantage from your fresh product that you can take advantage of. People tend to compare a new food with what they are familiar with. Once your family and friends get used to the fresh ground and fresh baked foods, they will be spoiled.

In my personal practice, I strive for simplicity and efficiency of time. I rarely bake standard loaves of bread. Instead, I cook pan bread in an iron skillet. Why? Because it is quick and I only make a quantity that I will use in a day or two so it is always fresh. Sprouting and rising sourdough takes a bit of organization, but only a small amount of time.

I used only whole wheat flours that I grind myself. I used or created recipes that use only a bare minimum of ingredients for simplicity. You can get a lot more complicated, but you can't do it with less effort. Simplicity is achieved without sacrifice of quality. When I make sourdough pan bread, there are no left-overs.

The information presented here has been simplified, tried, and proven. It uses only whole wheat grain and flours and a minimum of ingredients. It combines wheat and legumes for optimum protein utilization and emphasizes sprouting to create and increase vitamin content.

Purchasing whole grain wheat in bulk is relatively inexpensive. Local sources are preferred because of the shipping costs. By the time wheat reaches the grocery store shelf as bread, pastries, and breakfast cereal, it will cost you from about 4 to 20 times the cost of the whole grain. Wholesale and retail markups, processing, packaging, and transportation, combine to dramatically increase cost. While the food industry does offer convenience, for a price, using whole grains is not really inconvenient, once you have acquired the necessary skills, habits, and knowledge.

Sprouting dramatically increases the nutritional value of any grain or legume. Some B vitamins increase by as much as 1000% and vitamin C and vitamin A are created where none existed before.

Why the World Lives on Grain

Many books have been written on creating the optimum diet for your body type or blood type. The theory is that the diets of our ancestors affected our genetics and that a diet similar to that of our ancestors is likely to be optimum for us as well.

Here is a thumbnail sketch of recent human history. During the end of the last ice age, around the period of 10,000 B.C. to 18,000 B.C., there were fairly rapid and dramatic changes in climates and ecosystems.

As far as we know, the majority of our ancestors were part of a primitive nomadic hunter-gather culture. The hunter-gatherers lived on the "cave man" diet. That is, they ate everything edible that they could find. That included plants, animals, fish, etc. A particular ecosystem can only sustain a limited number of humans in this manner. As populations increased, some humans began domesticating animals, for meat, dairy, wool, and skins.

Controlling herds of animals was more efficient than hunting. The curly bashar horse from Mongolia is known as a superior forager. It provided the tribesmen with milk, wool, meat, and transportation. Goats, cattle, yaks, llamas, sheep, camels, and other animals are all used in similar fashion by nomadic herdsmen. This evolution allowed for higher population densities of humans and the evolution of a more stable culture.

Nomadic cultures developed around herding herbivorous animals. A nomadic culture, by nature, has limited possessions because it is always on the move and cannot carry many material possessions. In addition, the time and attention of its members are occupied by daily survival and domestic life. There is not much time available for the development of art, architecture, literature, etc. There are small surviving bands of herder cultures in Africa and other areas which have not changed for thousands of years.

As the climate and ecosystem stabilized and warmed, human populations began to grow and the demand for food grew as well. In areas suitable for farming, the cultivation of cereal grains and other crops increased the food supply dramatically. This allowed a much higher density of human population, and more organized, and more controlled, cultures. It was the wheat and barley fields that enabled the building of the cities of the Fertile Crescent and ancient Egypt.

From a nutritional and physiological perspective, a grain based diet is very different from an animal protein based diet. Some authors have proposed that humans evolved different physiological types based on the diets of their ancestors, with some being more adapted to grains, some dairy and some to a "hunter-gather" mix. There may be some truth in this.

Nevertheless, this planet runs directly or indirectly on a grain based diet, driven by economic considerations. It is possible to feed more people by growing grain than by living as hunter-gatherers. Wheat is less expensive to produce than beef.

The Different Types of Grain

Wheat

Wheat is a cereal grain, a type of grass. It is an annual plant and thus requires replanting each year. There are perennial forms of wheat that do not require replanting but they are rare and the crop yield is not as high as the annual types. Wheat has been genetically altered and selectively bred over many thousands of years to yield a large seed head with many plump seeds.

There are thousands of varieties of wheat adapted to different climates and having different properties. Wheat varieties are roughly classified as hard and soft types. In general, the hard types of wheat contain starch with larger grain size and higher gluten (protein) content than a soft variety. Gluten is the vegetable protein found in wheat and provides the body and texture that is necessary to form good loaves of bread. The soft types of wheat contain starch with smaller grain size and lower protein content.

The hard types are used for bread and the soft types are used for pastry. The flour from soft wheat is called pastry flour. A type of hard red wheat called durum is used to make pasta. The red types, which are generally the hard types, prefer the relatively dry climate of the grassy plains while the white types prefer the wetter climates that have a high rainfall.

Grains that have hulls, which include most varieties of rice, oats, barley, and buckwheat, require additional processing to remove the hull. Once the hull is removed, the shelf life of the grain is diminished. Wheat is desirable because it does not have a hull that requires extra milling and its shelf life is not compromised by milling.

Wheat is a first choice for food storage and self-sufficiency for several reasons:

- Wheat is high in protein, typically in the 13% to 20% range.

- Wheat protein is high in gluten, which enables it to make quality bread.

- Wheat stores well.

- Wheat is widely grown and relatively inexpensive when purchased as a whole grain.

You can and should regard the other grains as partially interchangeable with wheat in the recipes. Oats, triticale, millet, corn, amaranth, buckwheat, sorghum, rye, and rice flours can be added to wheat to make different flavors and textures of bread, pancakes, and biscuits.

Individuals who store food as a reserve in case of emergencies often store quantities of wheat because of its versatility, nutrition content, bread making qualities, and good storage qualities.

Rye

Rye is another cereal grain that resembles wheat. It is much hardier than wheat and will grow in areas that are too cold for wheat. Rye is traditionally grown in central and Eastern Europe and wild forms are found in central and eastern Turkey. Rye is used as a cooked cereal, flour for rye bread and in fermented form to make beer, whiskey and vodka.

Rye contains less protein than wheat and does contain gluten. It will make bread, but it is much heavier than bread made from wheat. Rye bread including pumpernickel and crisp bread is widely eaten in Northern and Eastern Europe.

For bread making, wheat flour is often combined with rye flour. Rye has a reputation for being able to grow on soil that is too poor to produce wheat and other grains. It appears that the nutritional content varies with the soil that it is grown on as well.

Triticale

Triticale is a true hybrid between wheat and rye. As a general rule, triticale combines the high yield and grain quality of wheat with the disease and environmental tolerance of rye. It has high enough gluten content for bread making and it possesses a superior quality protein.

Barley

Barley is a highly adaptable cereal grain with varieties adapted to growing conditions from the Arctic Circle to the tropics. It is high yielding and contains about 11 to 12 percent protein and does contain gluten. It has a short growing season and is somewhat drought tolerant. It is planted as a summer crop in northern climates and as a winter crop in tropical or subtropical climates. It is grown as a staple in Tibet where roasted barley flour is called "tsampa". It is used as a rice substitute, cooked in soups and stews where it is particularly delicious, made into bread, cooked as a hot cereal and fermented into beer.

Most barley has a hull around the seed that has to be milled off. There are a few varieties of hulless barley. De-hulled barley has the bran and germ intact whereas pearled barley has had the bran removed. De-hulled barley will not keep as well as barley with the hull intact.

Eating whole grain barley helps regulate blood sugar for up to 10 hours after consumption. Some sources indicate that whole grain barley has a low glycemic index, meaning that blood sugar is increased more slowly than most other carbohydrates thereby reducing sugar handling stress.

Oats

Oat varieties contain between 12-24% protein, the highest among cereal grains. The oat protein is mostly a globulin or legume like protein similar in quality to soy protein. There is some discrepancy among sources as to whether the oat contains gluten or not. It does contain a protein called avenin which some individuals can be sensitive or allergic to.

The oat contains a class of complex carbohydrates called betaglucans which are recognized for reducing blood cholesterol.

Oats also have a hull that must be removed by milling. Here, again, there are a few varieties of hulless oats. This is important if you are growing your own for food.

The oat is grown in temperate climates. It has a lower summer heat requirement and a greater tolerance for rain than most other cereal grains.

Oats are used as a rolled grain and cooked as in oatmeal and for making bread, cookies and cakes. Oats can also be used like barley in soups and as a rice substitute. Rolled oats can also be eaten raw.

Buckwheat

Buckwheat is a short season grain that is adapted to high altitude and low fertility or acidic soils. Too much fertilizer, especially nitrogen, will actually reduce its yield. Buckwheat is grown extensively in China, Russia, Ukraine and to some extent in Eastern Europe and Brazil. Buckwheat is unrelated to the wheat family (which includes rye, oats and triticale). Buckwheat is an herb that is related botanically to rhubarb and sorrel.

Buckwheat has a protein content of around 18% with a protein quality of 90%. The high quality of buckwheat protein is due to the high concentration of all of the essential amino acids. Buckwheat protein is gluten free.

Buckwheat seeds have a hull which must be removed by milling. The hulled seeds are called "groats".
The groats can be cooked or roasted and used as a rice substitute. Buckwheat flour is also used to make noodles called "soba" by the Japanese, "guksu" by the Koreans and "pizzocheri" by northern Italians. Farina made from groats

14

is used as a breakfast food or cereal and as a thickener in soups. Buckwheat pancakes, often raised with yeast, are eaten in several countries.

In addition to use as a seed grain, buckwheat groats can be sprouted and used as sprouts. Young buckwheat plants are often grown and eaten as a vegetable either raw or cooked. Buckwheat greens are especially high in Rutin.

Buckwheat contains no gluten and can be eaten by individuals with celiac disease or wheat allergy. Buckwheat does contain some substances to which some individuals have demonstrated food allergies. This is true of many if not all common foods.

Rice

Rice is a grain that is a major staple across the entire planet, especially in Asia. There are approximately 100,000 different varieties of rice in the world gene banks. Rice cultivation requires a warm or tropical and wet climate for cultivation. There are also some varieties that have been developed for dry land cultivation. Rice grains have a hull which must be removed by milling before it is eaten. Rice is used as a staple carbohydrate and is estimated to provide about one fifth of the calories consumed world wide.

The protein content is relatively low, approximately one third to one half of the protein content of wheat, oats, barley or buckwheat. It is also an incomplete protein in that it is deficient in some essential amino acids. This is true of most grains with the exception of buckwheat. This imbalance in amino acids can be corrected by combining grains with legumes. Rice protein is gluten free.

Rice has a hull which has to be removed by milling. What comes out of the hull is brown rice. Additional milling can remove the rice bran and germ and most of the oil in the rice leaving white rice. Removing the hull decreases the shelf life of the rice. Removing the bran, germ and oil drastically increases the shelf life of the rice but also removes oils, B vitamins, minerals and other nutrients that are rather important. Enriched rice is white rice with a few of the missing nutrients replaced by synthetic B vitamins.

Raw rice can be ground into flour and made into rice noodles and used in baked goods. Rice seeds can be boiled or steamed to make the familiar side dish or further fried in cooking oil or butter and combined with other ingredients to make fried rice.

Unhulled rice can also be soaked and sprouted to make sprouts or rice grass for use as a vegetable. This is not generally done because rice sprouts are lacking in culinary qualities.

Corn

Corn is the highest yielding and one of the most versatile of the grains. It will yield two to three times as many bushels per acre as wheat. Its protein content, however, is only about half that of wheat. There are hard flint corns, soft flour corns, sweet corns, hominy corns, and popcorns. Cornbread is excellent, easy to make and versatile. Corn meal, or flour, does not contain any gluten and will not rise like wheat flour. Corn is one of the easiest grains to plant, harvest, and handle for the home grower. The ears and seeds are large and can be easily planted, harvested and handled by hand. There is also no hull around the seeds that requires milling to remove.

The protein content of corn is similar to rice, about one half to one third that of wheat and similar grains. Corn protein is generally deficient in the essential amino acids lysine and tryptophan which can be supplemented by combining corn with legumes.

While corn and corn products are a good food source for those with gluten intolerance, there are some individuals who have corn allergies or sensitivities.

Corn was planted by Native Americans in hills in combination with beans and squash. The corn provided support for the beans and the nitrogen fixing rhizobia bacteria in the roots of the beans provided nitrogen to the corn and squash. The squash vines covered the ground with a thick cover of leaves that choked out weeds and limited loss of moisture through evaporation. The beans provided the amino acids and B vitamins that the corn lacked and the three foods together provided a balanced diet. This system of interplanting was used on the family farm of my youth in the Missouri Ozarks.

Ground corn seeds, or cornmeal, is a staple food in many cultures and regions. Porridge made from cornmeal has many names including polenta (Italy), mush or grits depending on the coarseness of the grind (USA), angu (Brazil), etc. Tortillas are made from masa. Masa is cornmeal made from corn treated with lime water. The whole kernels of lime treated corn are called Hominy. Corn bread and its variations were a staple food for Native Americans and early settlers in the Americas.

Diets dependent on unprocessed corn may experience a disease called pellagra which is caused by a deficiency of the B vitamin Niacin. Native Americans never had this problem. One reason is that they processed their corn into hominy and masa by soaking it in an alkali solution made from either lime (calcium hydroxide) or wood ashes (potassium hydroxide). The alkali treatment makes the niacin more available. It also appears to make the amino acids lysine and tryptophan more available improving protein quality. Corn stored as grain in a food storage plan should be alkali processed into hominy or masa for best nutritional results.

When corn is harvested in the immature or "green" stage, the kernels are soft and contain a relatively high sugar content rather than starch. Corns genetically selected to have higher sugar content in the "green" stage and to prolong the period of optimum sugar content are called sweet corn. Field or flour corns can also be harvested and used as sweet corn but the interval of optimum sweetness is relatively short and the ears must be cooked immediately on harvest to prevent the sugars from converting to starches.

Other varieties include flint, dent, and popcorns. All of them keep well when they have been properly dried. As a general rule of thumb, the flint varieties make better corn meal and hominy as they have a harder texture than the dent corns which make better flour. If you intend to make corn masa for tortillas and tamales, then the dent type is preferred. Popcorn can also be ground into meal or flour.

To be at its most pop able, popcorn needs to have moisture content between 13.5%-15.5% which makes it too moist for ideal storage. A small amount of drying will need to be done before it's packed away. It can be re-hydrated by sprinkling a small amount of water on the kernels and allowing it to be absorbed.

Millet

MIllet is a small seeded grain that makes flour with an appearance and taste similar to corn but finer in texture. It is very easy to mill into flour with a hand mill. It is also easy to grow and harvest and is suitable for small farmers or the gardener who wants to expand into producing their own cereal grains. Millet will tolerate dry climates better than most other grains.

The protein content of millet is about 11% by weight and is relatively rich in sulfur containing amino acids which make it a superior complement to legume proteins. Millet does not contain any gluten. Millets are also rich in many vitamins and minerals. However, millets do contain a mild thyroid peroxidase inhibitor and probably should not be consumed in large quantities by individuals with thyroid disease or on an iodine deficient diet. Sprouting the grain before cooking may improve this situation, but I am not aware if that has been scientifically proven or not.

Amaranth

Amaranth is an herb that grows widely as a weed and is cultivated for both as a green vegetable and a seed grain. The grain varieties yield abundantly, are easily grown and harvested and are tolerant of dry climates. One stalk of

18

grain amaranth may have a seed head that weighs over two pounds and contains over a half million seeds.

Amaranth protein content equals or exceeds wheat and oats and contains a high quality balance of essential amino acids. Amaranth contains no gluten. Some studies have shown that regular amaranth consumption reduces blood pressure and cholesterol while improving antioxidant status and immune function.

Quinoa

Quinoa, a species of goosefoot, is not a member of the grass family and not a true grain. Some varieties are grown for their edible seed. Other varieties are grown as a source of greens. The seeds possess an alkaline coating which has to be removed to make them edible. The presence of the alkaline coating discourages birds from eating the seeds before harvest. The removal process involves soaking the seed in several changes of water to wash out the alkali. Most commercial food sources have already been processed and can be cooked and eaten without any additional preparation.

The protein content is high, 12-18%, and high in quality containing a good balance of essential amino acids. Quinoa contains no gluten.

Quinoa cooks very quickly, has a light fluffy texture and a mild slightly nutty taste. It sprouts very quickly, in only 2-4 hours dramatically increasing its vitamin content. It can be treated as a substitute for rice, couscous or corn grits. It does possess vastly super nutritional value compared to these foods, especially when sprouted before cooking.

Legumes

Legumes are a good non-animal source of protein. In addition, the amino acid profile of legumes generally complements the amino acid profiles of grains so that the combination offers a more complete and more usable protein. Most legumes have protein contents ranging from 20%-35%. In cultures all over the world, it is common to find the two served together at a meal, making a complete protein, even when those doing the serving have no understanding of nutrition at all.

The legume family, of which all beans, peas, lentils, and peanuts are a part of, is one of the largest in the plant kingdom. The variety of edible legumes available to us is huge. The variety of colors, shapes, sizes, flavors and climactic adaptations is vast. In spite of this incredible variety of names and colors, legumes are largely interchangeable in cooking usage, although some dishes just wouldn't be the same if a substitute is used.

Legumes contain anti-nutrients and anti-vitamins which are destroyed by cooking. Legumes should never be eaten raw. The only exception is sweet lupine.

Below is a partial list of a few of the more commonly eaten bean varieties here in the U.S.

Black Bean

The black bean or turtle bean is a small, dark-brownish black, oval-shaped bean. They are used in Cuban, South and Central American and Chinese cuisine
They tend to bleed very darkly when cooked so they are not well suited to being combined with other foods, lest they give the entire pot a dark appearance.

Black Eyed Pea

The black eyed pea has many varieties of field peas eaten throughout the Southern United States. Black-eyed peas are small and oval-shaped with an overall creamy color and a distinctive black-eye. Dried field peas cook very quickly and are delicious with either rice or cornbread.

Garbanzo Bean

The garbanzo bean, chick pea or cecci pea (or bean) tends to be a creamy or tan color, rather roundish and larger than dried garden peas. Garbanzo beans are the prime ingredient in hummus and falafel. They are one of the oldest cultivated legume species known, going back as far as 5400 B.C. in the Near East.

Kidney Beans

Kidney beans also come in a large variety. They are used in chili and are prominent in Mexican, Brazilian and Chinese cuisine. They are toxic in the dry state and must be cooked. When cooked, they are delicious and nutritious.

Lentils

Lentils are distinctive from either beans or peas. They are roundish little discs with colors ranging from muddy brown, to green to bright orangish-red. They cook very quickly and have a distinctive flavor. They are used extensively in Chinese and Indian cuisine.

Lima Beans

Lima beans or butter beans are one of the most common beans found in the United States. They are available in large and small seeded varieties and bush and pole types. They originated in the Andean and Mesoamerican regions.

Lima beans are high in protein and fiber and contain carbohydrates that are digested slowly. This prevents blood sugar levels from rising too rapidly after eating them. They can therefore help balance blood sugar levels while providing steady, slow-burning energy, which makes them a good choice for people with diabetes suffering with insulin resistance.

Peanuts

The peanut, or groundnut, is not actually a nut at all, but a legume. Peanuts are a type of pea which flowers above ground then drops its pods into the earth to develop. Peanuts are high in both protein and fat. They are used for oil, peanut butter, boiled and roasted. Many Central and South American, African, Thai and Chinese dishes incorporate peanuts as a principal ingredient in their cuisine.

Pinto Bean

The pinto bean is one of the most commonly eaten beans in the US, especially in the Southwest. Pintos have a flavor that blends well with many foods.

Soybeans

Soybeans have both high protein and high oil content. Soybeans are small, and round with a multitude of different shades. While there are culinary varieties of soybean, most of the soybeans grown in the US are used as animal feed, exported or processed into a variety of food products. Soybean products include tofu, tempeh, textured vegetable protein, soy sauce, miso and hundreds of others. Although they are very high in protein, they don't lend themselves well to just being boiled until done and eaten the way other beans and peas do.

If you plan on keeping some as a part of your storage program you would be well served to begin to learn how to process and prepare them now when you're not under pressure to produce.

Like all other legumes, soybeans contain anti-nutrients that must be deactivated by cooking, sprouting or processing. Flour from uncooked soybeans cannot be added to bread mixes without negatively affecting the overall nutrition.

The Asian cultures where the soybean is native tend to process the beans by fermentation into miso, soy sauce, tempeh and similar foods.

White Beans

The small, white navy bean, also called pea bean or haricot is popular in Britain and the US. It is commonly used in baked beans, bean pies and bean soups. A different kind of white bean including Cannellini is popular in Central and Southern Italy.

Peas

The pea is a green, pod-shaped vegetable, widely grown as a cool season vegetable crop. The plants grow best at temperatures of 13 to 18 °C (55 to 64 °F). They do not thrive in the summer heat of warmer temperate and lowland tropical climates but do grow well in cooler high altitude tropical areas. Many cultivars reach maturity about 60 days after planting. Generally, peas are to be grown outdoors during the winter. While most peas are eaten as a green vegetable, they were grown as a dry pea in the past. Variations include edible podded peas and snow peas which are eaten as a cooked green vegetable.

Fava Beans

The fava bean or broad bean has a long tradition of cultivation going back to 6000 BC or earlier. They are native to North Africa and Southwest Asia and cultivated worldwide. The broad bean is very cold hardy and is often grown as a winter crop.

Broad beans are rich in tyramine and thus should be avoided by those taking monoamine oxidase inhibitors.

Raw broad beans contain vicine, isouramil and convicine which can cause hemolytic anemia in patients with hereditary susceptibility. This potentially fatal condition is called "favism" after the fava bean.

Broad beans are rich in L-dopa. L-dopa is the precursor to the neurotransmitters dopamine, norepinephrine, and epinephrine. Some also use fava beans as a natural alternative to drugs like Viagra, citing a possible link between L-dopa production and the human libido.

Sweet Lupin

The lupin is a legume that grows over multiple wide geographic areas. Many cultures have and do harvest lupin for food. Most lupins contain toxic bitter alkaloids which must be removed by leaching. There are some lupine strains that have been selected for low concentrations of the toxic bitter alkaloids. These lupins are referred to as sweet lupins. Newly bred variants of sweet lupins are grown extensively in Germany, the Northern US and other regions. They lack any bitter taste and require no soaking in salt solution. The seeds are used for different foods including vegetarian meat substitutes, lupin tofu and high protein lupin flour.

There are several things about the lupine that make it unique. First, it has a protein content and quality that is comparable to soybeans. Second, it favors cool weather while the soybeans require hot weather. Lupine will survive freezes down to 16 degrees F. Third, lupine does not have the digestive enzyme inhibitors present in soybeans. It can therefore be eaten or used as flour without heat treatment. While lupine seed cooked as a bean is rather tasteless, the flour adds valuable nutrition to pasta and baked products. Lupins are becoming increasingly recognized as an alternative to soy.

Lupine is grown in the northern United States, Northern Europe, and Russia as a summer crop and in the gulf coastal states and similar areas of the world as a winter crop. Lupine flour is an ideal protein complement for wheat flour.

Nutritional Considerations

The goal is to not just survive but be healthy. That extends to daily practices during good times as well as challenging times.

While grains and legumes form the nutritional basis of most of the population of this planet, they also contain some negative nutritional elements.

Anti-Nutrients

Antinutrients are compounds that interfere with the absorption of nutrients. Nutrition studies focus on those antinutrients commonly found in food sources. Antinutrients exist for a reason that is usually associated with the survival of the grain or legume seed. For example, enzyme inhibitors commonly found in legumes protect the raw legume seeds from the digestive system of the animal that ate the seed. The undigested legume seed then passes through the digestive tract and gets deposited in a blob of natural fertilizer where it can germinate and perpetuate its species. Human agriculture and culinary practices completely change this game, but we have to be aware that the primitive survival mechanism is still in play.

Anti-Nutrients in Legumes

In humans, the presence of these anti-digestion defenses poses a serious problem. Heating the legumes destroys these anti-digestion and anti-nutrition compounds. Inadequately cooked legumes can actually have a negative nutritional effect.

Adding flour from raw beans or soybeans to bread making recipes could be harmful. The baking process is usually not sufficient to deactivate the harmful substances in legumes. Sprouting and fermentation also reduce or eliminate the anti-nutrition in legumes.

Phytates

Phytic acid is found within the hulls or bran of seeds, nuts and grains. Phytic acid has a strong binding affinity to important minerals such as calcium, magnesium, zinc and iron. When a mineral binds to phytic acid, it becomes insoluble, precipitates and will be nonabsorbable in the intestines. Phytic acid also binds to the B vitamin niacin, potentially contributing to a deficiency of this vitamin and causing the deficiency disease, pellagra.

Several steps can be used to reduce or eliminate the negative effects of phytic acid. They include:

- Cooking alone will reduce phytic acid content to a degree.

- Sprouting reduces phytic acid content.

- Lactic acid fermentation reduces phytic acid content.

- Probiotic bacteria that live naturally in the intestinal tract produce a phytase enzyme that breaks down the phytic acid salts and liberates the nutritional minerals.

Flavonoids

A common food constituent is the flavonoids which include polyphenols, some of which have very positive health benefits and others which have antinutritional effects. Some of these compounds chelate essential trace elements and interfere with their absorption. Some may inhibit digestive enzymes and precipitate proteins. Some may have anticancer properties. Some may have anti-oxidant properties. Some may reduce cholesterol and improve heart and circulatory system health.

Given the complexity of this situation, the singular best advice is to have as varied a diet as possible.

Food Allergies

A food allergy is an adverse immune response to a food protein. An allergic reaction is distinct from a reaction to food toxins or food intolerance. Allergic reactions occur when the body's immune system mistakenly identifies a protein as harmful. Proteins or protein fragments that are not broken down in the digestive process provoke the creation of antibodies by the immune system. These antibodies fool the immune system into thinking that the protein is harmful and that the body is under attack. The immune system then initiates a reaction against the protein. Individuals with protein allergies commonly avoid contact with the problematic protein.

The gluten found in wheat and some other grains is one of the proteins that some individuals have difficulty with. Those individuals can use non-gluten containing grains as a direct substitute for wheat in most of the recipes in this book. The downside to substituting other grains for wheat is that gluten is what enables bread to rise and assume the familiar texture of leavened bread. Gluten is not the only potential offender, however. Any protein could be a problem for some individuals.

Typical signs of an allergic reaction include swelling of throat, lips or face, hives or vomiting. Anaphylaxis, which involves breathing problems or a drop in blood pressure, is a severe reaction which can be life-threatening.

Food intolerance, which can produce similar but generally less severe and more chronic symptoms, is caused by a variety of mechanisms. Some can be caused by immune system responses that are different from those caused by food allergies. Others are caused by a lack of digestive enzymes, like the enzyme lactase which digests milk sugar. Others may be caused by toxins.

A full discussion is beyond the scope of this text. Suffice it to say that one should identify food allergies and sensitivities and include in the diet and food storage only those foods that are not an issue. Professional help may be required if food allergies or sensitivities are suspected.

Some allergies manifest themselves only after a massive or prolonged exposure to the offending agent. Switching to a mostly wheat based diet would be one example. This makes it desirable to broaden the diet to include as many different grains, legumes and other foods as possible. It also emphasizes the importance of eating the same foods that you store. If you have any allergies or food sensitivities, it is best to learn about them sooner than later.

The manifestation of allergic responses is also frequently associated with stress levels. When stress levels increase, allergy symptoms may begin to manifest themselves. When stress levels diminish, allergy symptoms may diminish or disappear.

Sprouting seeds may also help diminish allergic reactions as well. The sprouting process breaks down some of the substances which some people may develop sensitivities to.

Testing Yourself for Food Allergies

There is one low tech food allergy test that you can do yourself. Dr. Arthur F. Coca developed the Coca Pulse Test for allergy elimination in the 1970's. It is based on the principle that foods to which you are intolerant are stressful to your body and will speed up your pulse.

The Pulse Test Procedure

For 3 days you will be taking your pulse 14 times per day.

- Once before you get out of bed
- Once before each meal
- 3 times after each meal at 30 minute intervals
- Just before you go to bed.

All pulses should be taken sitting, except the important one upon waking. Write down your results, and record what you eat at each meal. For best accuracy, avoid snacks, but if you succumb make a note of what you ate. It is extremely important that you take a full 1 minute pulse. Do not smoke during the 3 day test, as smoking affects results. This test may not work if you are taking a medical drug to control your heart rate, such as a beta-blocker. More details can be found in <u>The Pulse Test: The Secret of Building Your Basic Health</u> by Arthur F. Coca, M.D.

You can characterize your pulse as follows:

- Determine your <u>daily low pulse rate</u>. Normally this will be your waking rate, unless you are sleeping on something you are allergic to!

- Note the highest and lowest pulse on each day. The differential is the difference between the daily low and high rates. The average is the sum of the high and low divided by two. The maximum normal range difference is 16 beats. If your rate is higher than this, you may allergic to something.

- Once you have your average pulse, and your differential, anything that causes you to vary from that is suspect.

- Therefore, taking your pulse after each meal will enable you to tell whether something in your diet is increasing your pulse rate, indicating sensitivity.

- When you encounter a high pulse rate, eliminate an item from the preceding meal and test again. This may help you to identify the offending substance.

Disclaimer

This is a test, not a diagnosis. Carefully record your results and discuss them along with your concerns with your doctor.

The Freshness Factor

Freshly ground flour decays and spoils very quickly. The primary reason for this is the oxidation of essential oils and vitamins in the germ. In feeding studies conducted in Germany in 1970, rats were fed diets consisting of 50% flour or bread. Group 1 consumed fresh stone-ground flour. Group 2 was fed bread made with this flour. Group 3 consumed 15 day old flour. Group 4 was fed bread made with the flour fed to group 3. A fifth group consumed white flour.

After four generations, only the rats fed fresh stone-ground flour and those fed the bread made with it maintained their fertility. The rats in groups 3 to 5 had become infertile. Four generations for rats is believed to be equivalent to one hundred years in humans.

Some sources suggest that whole wheat flour can be left on the counter for 3-5 days, in the refrigerator for 10 days or in the freezer for 30 days. Other sources suggest that rancidity has been detected after only 2 days.

What is in the wheat germ? It is the embryo of the wheat. It contains protein, octacosanol, essential fatty acids, fatty alcohols, phosphorus, thiamin, zinc, magnesium, folic acid and vitamin E. In fact, it is one of the most concentrated food sources of vitamin E. The oil contains 55% Linoleic acid (omega-6), 16% palmitic acid, 14% oloeic acid and 7% Linolenic acid (omega-3). Octacosanol has been studied as a physical performance enhancing agent.

Prudence requires that flour should be used when ground and ground when used for best results.

Checking for Rancidity in Grains and Flour

It is the oil in the germ of the grain that becomes rancid after the grain is ground. How can you tell if flour is rancid or has gone bad? The low tech methods are smell and taste. Rancid oil and rancid flour will begin smelling like old gym socks. The taste will loose its sweetness and become increasingly bitter.

The Effects of Grinding, Refining and Adulteration

Modern milling technology makes the separation of bran, germ and endosperm easy. Whole wheat flour is produced by recombining ground bran with endosperm flour, but the germ is left out, because the oils in it would go rancid. Home ground flour still contains the germ with its superior nutritional content and vulnerability to oxidation and rancidity.

In the 1940s, a flour enrichment program was instituted to compensate for nutrients removed by milling flour. In the 'enriched' flour only the B vitamins thiamin, riboflavin, and niacin and the mineral, iron, were added, in amounts approximately equivalent to those removed from whole wheat. Approximately 20 other known nutrients were removed by milling and not replaced.

For centuries, bakers have known that 'good quality' baked goods could not be made with freshly milled flour, because the dough would lack strength and resilience to trap gas. Until the 20th century it was common practice to store flour for months to allow oxygen to condition it. Chemical oxidizing agents or bleaches were developed to produce the same aging effects in 24-48 hours. They cause oxidation of the gluten and bleaching of the yellowish carotene pigments which could have been sources of vitamin A.

Some of the bleaching agents used include: chlorine, chlorine dioxide, benzoyl peroxide, potassium bromate, ammonium persulfate, ammonium chloride, acetone peroxide, azodicarbonamide, ascorbic acid, l-cysteine and mono-calcium phosphate. The use of these agents has been the subject of considerable legal and legislative confrontation. While the use of these agents has been approved in the USA and Canada, it was not without opposition.

Note that one of the additives is potassium bromate. Bromium is one of the halide elements which include iodine. Bromide compounds can displace iodine and potentially contribute to clinical or subclinical iodine deficiency and associated thyroid problems.

Aflatoxins

It's long been known that eating moldy grain is bad for your health. The USDA and the various state departments of agriculture go to a great deal of trouble to detect grain and legumes infected with toxic fungi. The fungal type that has caused the most commotion in recent history is the various Aspergillus species of molds. Under certain conditions with certain grains, legumes and nuts infected with this fungus can produce a mycotoxin called "aflatoxin". This is a serious problem in some parts of the world, most especially in peanuts and occasionally in corn.

In addition to its toxicity, aflatoxin is also a very potent carcinogen (cancer causing agent). In addition to the Aspergillus molds, there is a large family of molds called Fusarium that can produce a wide variety of mycotoxins.

If you observe mold growth in your whole grains, or other grain products, they should be discarded. Most mycotoxins are not broken down or destroyed by cooking and there is no safe way to salvage grain that has molded.

The easiest method to prevent mold growth in your stored grains and legumes is simply to keep them too dry for the mold to grow. The Aspergillus and Fusarium molds require moisture contents of 18% and above to reproduce.

If you are storing raw (not roasted) peanuts, in the shell or shelled, you want to get the moisture content to less than 8% as peanuts are particularly susceptible to mold growth. The recommended moisture content for all other grain and legume storage is no more than 10%.

Danger – Warning!!

The mycotoxins from moldy grain can kill you. Grains can develop mold when the moisture content is too high. Check your grain sources and the moisture content of your grain very carefully.

Enhancing Wheat Based Nutrition

There are two steps that one can take to increase the nutritional qualities of food prepared from wheat and other grains. First, one can combine grains with legumes to improve the amino acid mix and make the vegetable proteins more assimilable. Second, sprouting grains breaks down lignins, which some individuals are sensitive to, and creates vitamins that did not previously exist.

Wheat contains gluten which has a molecular characteristic that enables it to bind a bread dough together, stretch, and trap the carbon dioxide bubbles that are produced by the yeast used to make the bread rise. This makes chewy, fluffy, spongy, light, breads and pastries possible.

The protein in wheat, however, is not a complete protein. The human body requires the simultaneous presence of eight essential amino acids to be able to synthesize body tissue (human protein). Wheat contains some of the essential amino acids in generous quantities but is deficient in certain others. Without the proper ratio of amino acids, much of the wheat protein cannot be assimilated into human protein. The amino acid most lacking is Lysine. Lysine is found in large quantities in legumes. Combining wheat with legumes improves the amino acid balance dramatically and makes the proteins in both much more assimilable by the human body. That is why the recipes in this book emphasize wheat/legume combinations. Diet for a Small Planet by Frances Moore Lappe is the classic reference on combining plant proteins. Please read this book.

The wheat to legume ratio should be about 4 to 1. Combining 3 cups of wheat with 1 cup of beans increases the usability of the proteins in both by about 33%.

While combining grain and legume proteins will provide an adequate quality and quantity of protein to supply the needs of the human body, certain other essential nutrients are still missing. What are missing are certain vitamins and minerals. By using a lot of sprouts, you can increase the amount of B vitamins dramatically and add vitamins A and C. There still may be insufficient amounts of vitamin A, vitamin C, and certain B vitamins, however.

There is also a lack of certain essential mineral elements such as calcium. The trace element content also depends on the soil that the grain was grown on. Many of the missing major and minor nutrients can be supplied by leafy green vegetables. Kale is an especially rich source of calcium, vitamin A, and other vitamins and minerals. To create a balanced diet, include as much variety as possible. If you have to survive on wheat and legumes, use sprouted grains and legumes as much as possible and take a balanced vitamin and mineral supplement.

Vitamin B12 is completely or nearly completely lacking in vegetable foods. This vitamin is produced by bacteria that live in the digestive tracts of some animals. Some animal proteins or B12 vitamin supplements are required to maintain health.

Adding Legumes to Increase Protein Utilization

Legumes are plants that have a symbiotic relationship with nitrogen fixing bacteria that live in their root system. The bacteria draw nutrients from the plant and, in turn, take nitrogen from the air and feed it to the plant in a form that the plant can use to make amino acids and proteins. Thus, legumes tend to be higher in protein than non-legume plants.

The legumes include all kinds of beans, English peas, fava beans, lentils, peanuts, soybeans, and sweet lupine.

34

Most legumes, with the exception of lupine, must be cooked before being consumed. It is important to combine properly prepared legumes with grains in order to optimize the amino acid ratios and improve protein assimilation. Plant proteins simply are not equal to animal protein for nutritional assimilation.

Food Combination

The important point to make here is that the digestion of starches and proteins involve different processes. The digestion of starches requires an alkaline environment. The process begins in the mouth with chewing and the introduction of the enzyme amylase in the saliva. About 10% of the starch is broken down in the mouth, if you chew your food well. The process stops when the food reaches the acid medium of the stomach and resumes again when the food leaves the stomach and enters the small intestine. The small intestine is again an alkaline environment.

Protein, on the other hand, requires the acid medium of the stomach to begin the breakdown and assimilation process.

The point of this is that it is easier for your body to absorb what you eat if you avoid combining a large amount of meat with a large quantity of starch. It is also advisable to avoid combining starches with acid foods such as fruits and some vegetables like tomatoes.

For a high protein meal, combine meat, fish, chicken or protein from gluten meat substitute (described in a later section) and TVP (Textured Vegetable Protein) or some other form of soy protein. As a complement to this type of meal, use salads and vegetables that are low in starch.

Most fruits are best eaten alone. Dried fruits can be taken as a snack either directly or stewed. Avoid refined sugar and artificial sweeteners.

The use of meats in noodles and dumplings should be limited to flavoring quantities only. Potatoes, carrots, other root vegetables, squashes and pumpkins, and green leafy vegetables combine well with wheat and grain foods. Green salads, cooked greens, green peas, green beans, sauerkraut, and other fermented vegetables combine well with meats.

Increasing Vitamin Content by Sprouting

If you were forced to live on a diet of wheat and beans, boredom would be the least of your difficulties. Nutritional deficiencies would be the real killer. True, you would be getting adequate quantities of protein but certain essential vitamins and minerals would be missing. Some of those vitamins can be supplied by sprouting the wheat and other grains and legumes in your diet. Some vitamins such as folic acid may increase by a factor of ten or more above what existed in the unsprouted grain. Other vitamins, such as vitamin A and C, will be created by sprouting where they did not exist before. Sprouting is valuable.

The process of sprouting also converts starches into sugars. Malt is made by sprouting grain then cooking it and extracting the sugar out. You can dry sprouted grain then cook it or grind it into flour to act as a sweetener in place of honey.

Cooked sprouted wheat can serve as a direct replacement for cooked wheat berries. This is advisable since the vitamin content is so dramatically increased. While sprouting doesn't create any minerals it does destroy the phytates that can bind with minerals making them unavailable to your body. Plant seeds contain proteins called lectins which bind the carbohydrates together. It is believed that these lectins may be a contributing factor in food sensitivity and food allergies. It is known that sprouting decreases the lectin content of the seeds.

Grain and Legume Storage

Do You Want Your Food Dead or Alive?

Grain and Legume seeds that are viable for sprouting are alive. The optimum storage conditions for live versus dead grains and grain products vary greatly in one respect. Dead foods must be protected from oxidation to extend shelf life while live foods require oxygen to remain alive.

If you want to sprout your grains and legumes, **do not** use oxygen absorbers, nitrogen flushing, mylar bags or other oxygen elimination methods.

If you are storing processed food, like dried or freeze dried fruits, vegetables, meats, milk, eggs, bulgur, pasta, etc. or grains with short shelf life like brown rice, rolled oats, oat groats, etc., **do** use oxygen eliminators like mylar bags, nitrogen flushing and oxygen absorbers.

All foods, alive or dead, last much longer at lower temperatures and lower moisture content.

Shelf Life of Grains and Legumes

Most shelf life labels or listed expiration dates are used as guidelines based on normal handling of products. Use prior to the expiration date does not necessarily guarantee the safety of a food or drug, and a product is not always dangerous or ineffective after the expiration date.

For Dead Food (Non-Sproutable Grains and Seeds)

These estimates below are for hermetically sealed, **oxygen free** containers stored at **65 degrees F (18 degrees C) or below.** The storage container could be a sealed No. 10 can or a food grade polyethylene bucket with a mylar liner. This assumes nitrogen flushing and the use of oxygen absorbers to remove oxygen. These figures are based on published estimates from several manufacturers.

For **Hard Grains** (Corn, Kamut, Millet, Durum wheat, Hard red wheat, Hard white wheat, Soft wheat, Spelt, Triticale), the storage life is estimated to be about **30 years**.

For **Soft Grains** (Hulled or Pearled Barley, Oat Groats, Rolled Oats, Quinoa, Rye) the storage life is estimated to be about **25 years**.

For **Pasta** the storage life is estimated to be about **20 years**.

For **Flour and Cracked Grains** (All Purpose Flour, Unbleached Flour, White Flour, Whole Wheat Flour, Cornmeal, Dehydrated Refried Beans, Cracked wheat, Oatmeal) the storage life is estimated to be about **5 years**.

For **Legumes** (Adzuki Beans, Black eye Peas, Black Turtle Beans, Garbanzo Beans, Great Northern Beans, Kidney Beans, Lentils, Lima Beans, Mung Beans, Pink Beans, Pinto Beans, Small Red Beans, Soy Beans, etc.) the storage life is estimated to be about **25 years**.

For **Brown Rice**, the storage life is estimated to be about **½- 1 year**.

For White Rice, the storage life is estimated to be about **25 years**.

For **Freeze Dried Fruits and Berries** the storage life is estimated to be about **20 years**.

For **Freeze Dried Vegetables** (Broccoli, Cabbage, Carrots, Celery, Onions, Peppers, Potatoes) the storage life is estimated to be about **20 years**.

For **Freeze Dried Dairy and Eggs** (Cheese Powder, Powdered Eggs, Butter Powder, Whey Powder) the storage life is estimated to be about **5-10 years**.

For **Non-Fat Dry Milk** the storage life is estimated to be about **20 years**.

For Live Food (Sproutable Seeds)

The following seed storage life estimates are derived from 18 years of experience by The Sprout People (http://www.sproutpeople.com/). This is their estimate of what one can expect when the seeds are stored under cool (55-70 degrees F) (13-21 degrees C) and low humidity (70% or less) conditions. Cooler and drier will produce better results.

Seed	Shelf Life	Seed	Shelf Life
Adzuki	5 Years	Alfalfa	4 Years
Barley	2 Years	Black Bean	5 Years
Buckwheat	2 Years	Flax, Brown	3 Years
Flax, Golden	3 Years	Garbanzo	5 Years
Hemp Seed	5 Years	Kamut	2 Years
Lentil	5 Years	Millet	5 Years
Mung Bean	5 Years	Oats	2 Years
Pea	5 Years	Peanut	5 Years
Pinto Bean	5 Years	Popcorn	8 years
Quinoa	3 Years	Rice	3 Years
Rye	2 Years	Soy Bean	4 Years
Spelt	2 Years	Sunflower	2 Years
Triticale	2 Years	Wheat	2 Years

Actual seed viability and storage life can vary greatly, depending on the grain, temperature, humidity and the quality of the crop.

I recently opened up some old stored wheat and germination tested the seed for viability. Hard red winter wheat that was 16 years old responded with a 94% germination rate. This was organic wheat from Montana with moisture content below 10%. It was stored in a five gallon food grade polyethylene bucket with a good seal. It was stored outdoors in a shaded shed. The temperature fluctuated with the seasons, but was generally cool and never hot. There were no oxygen absorbers, nitrogen flushing, mylar bags, etc.

Even cooler temperatures would have improved these results. The USDA states, "Each 5.6°C. (10.08°F) drop in temperature doubles the storage life of the seeds".
A constant cool temperature would also have helped. Seeds prefer a constant rather than fluctuating temperature.
Placing desiccant packs in the buckets would have lowered the moisture content even further and extended seed life as well.

While it is clearly possible to store good quality wheat and other seeds and grains for a very long under ideal conditions, it is best to rotate them frequently to keep them at their nutritional peak and eliminate waste.

Germination Testing

It is important to periodically test the viability of all of your stored seeds to insure that they are remaining viable. The procedure is simple.

(1)   Count out 100 undamaged seeds.

(2)   Soak the seeds for 12 hours in warm water.

(3)   Drain and let them set for 2-4 days in a warm place while keeping them moist but exposed to air.

(4)   Then count the number of seeds that have sprouted. This number is the germination rate.

Storage Containers

What you store your grains in is important. It must absolutely be moisture tight. You also want something that is unbreakable, reusable, able to withstand rough handling, stackable and of the right size.

Consider No. 10 metal cans. These cans are often used for food storage. Sealing the cans requires special equipment which is expensive but may be available through community kitchens or cooperatives. The cans are not reusable and their volume is low for grain storage.

Consider glass jars and jugs. They meet all of the desired characteristics except one. They are breakable.

Consider mylar bags. Mylar bags are made from a material that consists of layers of plastic and aluminum foil. The aluminum foil provides increased protection against oxygen penetration. They are lacking only in their durability if they are used alone. They can be added to other containers to provide an extra layer of protection for the stored food against moisture and oxygen.

Consider plastic food grade barrels. When filled, they are too heavy to move around easily. Otherwise, they are quite serviceable provided that the lids make a secure seal.

Then the three bears discovered food grade polyethylene buckets and they were jussst right. They come in 4, 5, and 6 gallon sizes. They can withstand rough handling; their weight is in a range that most people can lift and move; they are reusable; they are stackable; the gasketed lids make a moisture tight seal; no mylar bags or other enhancers are needed provided that the lids are in new condition and put on correctly.

Oxygen Absorbers

An oxygen absorber is a small packet of chemical that reacts with oxygen and "absorbs" the oxygen from the air in the container that it is placed in. Its purpose is to increase the shelf life of food. Some food components, such as vegetable oils, oxidize as a direct reaction with oxygen in the air. Fungus, yeast and aerobic bacteria also require oxygen. Placing an oxygen absorber in a food container inhibits oxidation and the growth of aerobic micro-organisms.

Note: Oxygen absorbers do not inhibit the growth of anaerobic micro-organisms.

Note: Oxygen absorbers react with the oxygen in the air to produce a chemical compound that is solid rather than gaseous. Removing the oxygen from the gaseous state will reduce the pressure inside the container by about 20%.

41

Your container must be strong enough or flexible enough to handle this partial vacuum. Alternately, nitrogen flush first. Nitrogen flushing will reduce the oxygen in the container and reduce the partial vacuum produced when the residual oxygen is taken up by the oxygen absorber.

Should you use oxygen absorbers in your food storage? That depends on whether you are storing live sproutable seeds, or "dead" food.

Live sproutable seeds require oxygen to stay alive. The amount that they consume is extremely small but not zero. Adding oxygen absorbers to sproutable grains and seeds is a very bad idea. For the same reason, the use of mylar bags is also not recommended. The plastic buckets will "leak" oxygen, but that is even desirable since you are storing live seeds. The mylar bags would block the leakage of oxygen.

Other foods, like powdered milk, powdered eggs, dried or freeze dried prepared foods, and mixes, and freeze dried or dehydrated fruits, vegetables and meats will all store better and longer if oxygen absorbers are used.

Desiccants

A desiccant is a substance which absorbs water vapor or water (moisture), thus removing it from the air within a contained area. Solid desiccant materials include silica gel, calcium sulfate, calcium chloride and others. Desiccant material is commonly available in packets, some of which contain an attached indicator. The indicator turns color when the material becomes saturated with water. Desiccants can be "regenerated" after they have become saturated by placing them in an oven at 200 degrees F or 100 degrees C.

Desiccants absorb water vapor from the air in storage containers and from the stored food. By doing so, they increase the shelf life of the stored food. This is true in all dry stored foods including living sproutable seeds and grains. The use of desiccants is highly recommended.

The rule of thumb is to use 4 to 8 ounces of desiccant for each 5 gallon bucket of grain or legumes.

An improvised moisture absorber can be made from a piece of wood. Place a piece of wood in the oven and dry it to "extreme bone dry" and place it in the container. It will, to some extent, absorb moisture from the inside of the container.

Moisture Content in Wheat

Wheat is marketed by weight. Therefore, it is not in the financial interest of a business to reduce the moisture content to less than that required for short to medium term storage. Reducing moisture content requires an expenditure of energy and the lower weight of drier grain reduces its monetary value. Both cost money. In contrast, long term storage requires the lowest moisture content that can be obtained. The commercial standard for wheat moisture content is 13.5%.

Moisture content in grain is vitally important for long term storage. It should be 10 percent or less. Wheat that is stored in cool, dry conditions will last for a very long time. Intact grains of wheat have been found in 4000 year old Egyptian tombs. Long term storage requires that you keep the grain both dry and cool.

Low moisture content reduces the seeds metabolism and extends its life. There is another concern, however, that is very serious. Each kernel of grain or bean may host thousands of fungi spores and bacteria. At moisture levels between 13.5% and 15% some fungal species are able to grow and reproduce. Other species require a moisture level in the 16-23% range. Aerobic bacteria require a moisture level of about 20%. Raw peanuts may have Aspergillus mold growth that produces aflatoxin at 8% moisture content or more. **Toxins from moldy grain can kill you.**

43

Measuring Moisture Content in Grain

To measure the moisture content in grain:

- Grind a small quantity into flour and weigh it.

- Weigh a glass dish, place the flour in it and heat it in the oven at a temperature of 130 degrees Celsius or 266 degrees Fahrenheit for 1 hour.

- Weigh the dried sample.

- Calculate the moisture content with the following formula:

Moisture content=((weight of sample)-(weight of dried sample))/(weight of sample)

Protecting Stored Wheat and Grains from Insects

Weevils are a potential problem with stored wheat. The moths lay their eggs on the seeds before they are harvested. Soon after harvest, they hatch into little worms that consume the grain. Some farmers and grain mill operators apply chemicals to the stored grain to kill the weevils. I do not trust the chemical methods and prefer not to eat wheat that has been treated by this method. Other methods of controlling weevils include heat treatment, fumigation with carbon dioxide and application of diatomaceous earth.

One half pound of dry ice will fumigate 100 pounds of grain. Place a few inches of grain in a container, place the dry ice on it, and fill the rest of the container.

You can accomplish the same thing with small quantities of grain by heating it to 150 degrees F (66 degrees C) for 20 minutes. This is usually enough to kill the weevil eggs with a negligible effect on the viability of the grain. Heating the grain is not the most desirable method of killing weevils, but I have used it successfully without any apparent loss of shelf life.

Another method of protecting grain against insects is to mix diatomaceous earth with it at the rate of <u>one cup to each 40 pounds of grain</u> (approximately 1 five gallon bucket).   It must be mixed very thoroughly in order to be effective.

Diatomaceous earth is a fine white powder consisting of the calcium skeletons of one celled organisms called diatoms. Under a microscope, one can see their tiny skeletons with long sharp spikes. These microscopic spikes puncture the soft skins of weevils causing them to leak body fluids and die. When cooked they simply add a small amount of calcium to the diet. This method has the advantage that diatomaceous earth can be stored and used when needed.   Dry ice, on the other hand, is very volatile and must be kept frozen until used.

Diatomaceous earth is approved by the USDA as an animal feed additive. Actually, there are two kinds of diatomaceous earth to be found on the market and only one of them is suitable for use in your stored grains. The kind that you **DO NOT WANT** is the type sold by swimming pool suppliers as a filtering agent. It is unsuitable for use with your foodstuffs. The type that you want is sold by a number of suppliers as a garden insecticide. Many organic garden suppliers will carry it. Read the label carefully to be certain no deleterious substances such as chemical pesticides have been added.

Some food storage companies advocate the use of nitrogen packing with stored grains. This should suffocate the weevils, but if the grains are kept dry and cool, the nitrogen should not be needed as a preservative. Remember, grains are alive. Even though they are dormant, respiration does occur although at a very low rate. They do need oxygen to stay alive. Dried or freeze dried foodstuffs are another matter. They benefit greatly from the oxygen free nitrogen atmosphere.

Selecting and Storing Wheat

If any local farmers in or near your area grow wheat, you can locate them by inquiring at a farm supply store. They will generally be happy to sell you wheat directly. You should ask the farmer what chemicals he uses on his crop. Farmers are practical and honest people. While few of them are truly organic, they are not prone to use chemicals that serve no purpose. If they are having problems with diseases or pests, they will use chemicals rather than loose their crops. Still, with a little work, you may be able to locate some organic farmers, and when you do, they will know others.

Look for wheat, grains and legumes that are:

(1) Organically grown
(2) Low moisture content
(3) High Protein
(4) Not treated with chemicals

Store your wheat in 4, 5, or 6 gallon food grade poly buckets with rubber gasketed lids or 55 gallon food grade plastic barrels with gasketed lids. Add diatomaceous earth at the rate of one cup per bucket of grain or legumes and mix thoroughly.

Before sealing the container, lay a 4 to 8 ounce bag of dry silica gel on top of the grain.

Selecting and Storing Other Grains

Oats, buckwheat, rice and barley normally have a hull around the seed. They will store well in the unhulled state but only very poorly after the hull has been removed. Most of the commercial forms used for human food have been hulled.

The hulls around the seeds are inedible and not easy for an individual to remove at home. Hulled seeds or "groats" must be rotated frequently or stored as "dead" food that cannot be sprouted since its shelf life is short. The storage method would then be to use mylar bags inside the container and use nitrogen flushing and oxygen absorbers to protect against rancidity of the oils in the grain.

An exception can be found in buckwheat. Hulled buckwheat will sprout. Kasha is usually toasted and will not sprout. Raw buckwheat is white/green to light brown while toasted buckwheat is medium brown. Unhulled buckwheat has a black hull and can be sprouted or grown in a garden or pot for greens. The hulls, however, are inedible. Buckwheat is high in protein and nutritious and worth the effort to store and eat. For live sprouting seeds, store the same way as wheat. The shelf life will be shorter, however.

Note – Wheat has no hull and stores very well. This is one reason that wheat excels as a core item for food storage.

Corn is another useful storage food. The seeds are hard, store well, have no hull to contend with and provide a versatile source of carbohydrates. Corn can be sprouted but is not very palatable. Processing corn with lime (calcium hydroxide) to make hominy or masa flour is desirable as it improves the nutritional quality of the corn. Storage of corn is similar to that of wheat.

Protein Content in Wheat

The protein content of wheat will vary widely with the climate, soil, and variety. Premium quality hard red spring wheat will have a protein content of 15% or higher. Wheat must have a minimum protein content of 13% to be considered acceptable for bread making. 13% is marginal and the higher the protein content, the better the dough will rise and hold its shape. There is no grading category for wheat above 16% protein content. As a result the really good stuff with 20% protein content gets mixed in with the rest in commercial distribution. This is another reason it is wise to determine the source and protein content of the wheat that you buy.

If you do acquire wheat of low protein content, it is still edible and can be used for pancakes, sprouts, and cereal. Bread made from it may not rise as well, however.

There are a number of resellers and brokers listed in the resource section. Your local food coop may be a good source for organic grains. When buying from a food coop, you should still check out their source and, if possible, determine the protein content and moisture content of the grain.

Making and Cooking Sprouts

Sprouting Wheat

This applies to rye, kamut, spelt and triticale as well as wheat. Soak wheat in warm water overnight. Drain and place the soaked wheat into a sprouting container. A large jar will serve as a sprouting container. Use a cloth or screen as a cover on the jar so that it can breathe. The sprouting wheat berries need oxygen. Either rinse three or four times per day or set up a drip watering system. The sprouts can be used when only 1/8 to 1/4 inch long. To test their readiness, eat a few raw to determine how sweet they are. When they are sweet, they are ready.

The time required will vary from 2 to 4 days depending upon temperature. The sprouting container must be well drained. A drip system can consist of a large plastic pop bottle with pinholes in the bottom suspended over a container that has drainage holes in its bottom.

Another method is to place the soaked wheat kernels on several layers of damp towel and cover them with several more layers of wet towel. The towel must be resaturated periodically and must be well drained. The towels should be washed and sterilized between batches. This can be done by placing the towel in hot water or drying it in an oven set to 300 degrees F (150 degrees C). Sterilizing the towels slows down the development of mold.

If your room temperature is cold, place the sprout containers inside a styrofoam beverage chest and place a couple jars of hot water inside with them. An optimum temperature for sprouting is around 85 degrees F (30 degrees C).

Sprouting Other Grains

Amaranth and quinoa sprouts are strong flavored and not a good choice for sprouting.

Barley and oats will only sprout if unhulled. The hulls are inedible so these are not the best choice for sprouting.

Buckwheat makes excellent sprouts. Use only hulled, raw buckwheat groats. Soak the seeds for only about 20 minutes. The cloth method is probably best but the jar and screen method will also work. The sprouts will be ready in 1-3 days depending on temperature.

Other Sprouting Seeds

Other seeds can be used to produce sprouts. Sprouts are like fresh vegetables.

Brassica family sprouts include cabbage, kale, cauliflower, broccoli, raab, and brussel sprouts. Soak the seeds for about 12 hours. The sprouts will be ready in 1-2 days.

Mustard family sprouts include the various varieties of mustard greens and Chinese cabbages. Soak the seeds for about 12 hours. The sprouts will be ready in 1-2 days.

For radish, soak the seeds for about 12 hours. The sprouts will be ready in 1-2 days. They are Spicy.

For sunflower sprouts, hulled sunflower seeds. At the end of the soak period, skim off the hulls to prevent spoilage. Soak the seeds for about 12 hours. The sprouts will be ready in 1-2 days. They have a decent flavor.

For onion seed sprouts, soak the seeds for about 12 hours. The sprouts will be ready in 1-2 days. They taste just like green onions.

Making Wheat Grass

You can use rye, triticale, spelt, and kamut interchangeably for this application. You can also use oats, barley, buckwheat or rice in the hull as well. Take a plastic seed planting tray that has drainage in the bottom and place fertile dirt in it that has been sterilized by baking in the oven (to kill the mold spores). In this, plant some wheat. It will germinate and send up green shoots. When about 3 to 4 inches tall, cut off the top two inches with scissors or a knife and use it as a raw or cooked vegetable or for juice.

Many People like to juice wheat grass to obtain its nutrients. In theory, you can get the same benefit by eating it whole. In practice, you will discover that it is very fibrous. Like all other grasses, it is edible but not choice. I have read stories of Chinese farmers who survived the famines caused by W.W.II by eating grass. I have also read stories that boiled grass was one of the menu items served in Siberian prison camps.

Several companies sell hand cranked juicers that can be used with wheat grass and other tender greens. The nutritional and rejuvenation qualities of these juices have earned them many advocates.

I recommend that you sprout buckwheat greens for use as a green vegetable. Buckwheat greens are grown for food in many parts of the world and are very high in rutin and other nutrients. They are also tender and tasty. Green vegetables produced in this way will acquire minerals from the soil. Enrich your soil mixture with granite dust, dolomite, and greensand.

Grinding Sprouted Wheat

Grinding sprouted wheat is different from grinding dry wheat. Ground sprouted wheat is soft, gooey, very sticky, and wet. It will immediately clog a stone grinder. Do not grind sprouted wheat with a stone grinder. Metal burr type mills work well, but they do get a bit gooey and require immediate cleaning after use. It helps a bit if you oil the interior parts and surfaces before doing the grinding.

Another method of grinding sprouts is to use a suribachi. A suribachi is a glass or porcelain mortar or bowl with a maze of sharp cutting indentations scored into it's inside surface. Combined with a wooden pestle, it can grind soft wet grains or soft dry seeds. The suribachi is useful for this purpose because it is easy to clean.

Another method of grinding wheat sprouts is to use a small hand cranked meat grinder. Use the blades and plates designed for a fine grind. The advantages of the meat grinder are that it is fast, and it is designed to come apart easily for cleaning. It doesn't change the fact that ground wheat sprouts are a gooey mess. It still helps to oil the parts before grinding. This is my **preferred** method of grinding wheat sprouts.

If you have more wheat sprouts than you can use, you can dry them. However, drying reduces the vitamin content, especially vitamin C. Fresh is preferable.

Legume Sprouts

You can sprout beans and peas but:

- In order to fully destroy the anti-nutrients, the sprouts need to be long (like the bean sprouts you see in the supermarket or oriental dishes).

- Many of the sprouts from beans taste like crap. The exceptions are sprouts from soybeans, lentils, peanuts, garbanzo beans, peas and mung beans.

Sprouting Legumes

Soy beans – Soak them in cool water for 8-12 hours until they are all soft. Thoroughly rinse them until you get clear water. Rinse and drain the seeds approximately every 4-8 hours until they reach a desirable length. Some like them short and others longer. I suggest that longer is better because it does a more thorough job of processing out the undesirable components in soybeans. The sprouting could take from 2 to 6 days. Soy sprouts should be cooked or at least blanched to destroy the trypsin inhibitors in the sprouts.

Mung beans - Soak them for 8-12 hours.   Rinse and drain the seeds approximately every 4-8 hours until they reach a desirable length. The sprouting can take from 1-6 days depending on the temperature and your preferred length of sprouts.

Garbanzos beans – Soak the beans for 12-18 hours. Rinse and drain the seeds approximately every 4-8 hours until they reach a desirable length. The sprouts will reach a desirable size in 2 to 4 days.

Peas - Black eye, field and crowder peas- Soak the seeds for 12-14 hours. Rinse and drain the seeds approximately every 4-8 hours until they reach a desirable length. The sprouts will reach a desirable size in 1 to 3 days.

Peanuts - Soak the seeds for 12-14 hours. Rinse and drain the seeds approximately every 4-8 hours until they reach a desirable length. The sprouts will reach a desirable size in 2 to 4 days. You must use raw, unblanched seeds. It is best to remove the skins by a brief preliminary soak and rubbing. Be cautious of discoloration that could be cause by aflatoxin producing mold. Peanuts are vulnerable to this mold.

Lentils - Soak the seeds for 8-14 hours. Rinse and drain the seeds approximately every 4-8 hours until they reach a desirable length. The sprouts will reach a desirable size in 1 to 2 days.

Alfalfa and Clover - Soak the seeds for 4-8 hours. , sprout 6-8 days. Rinse and drain the seeds approximately every 4-8 hours until they reach a desirable length. The sprouts will produce greens in 4 to 8 days.

Essene Bread

The Essenes were an ascetic community that had a marked influence on the early Christian church. It was an Essene community on the Dead Sea that buried the famous "Dead Sea scrolls."

The Essenes are credited with the technique and basic recipes for Essene bread. Essene bread is made from sprouted wheat and prepared at a low temperature. These two practices insure the maximum possible vitamin content for this foodstuff. The sprouting also breaks down the lectins and other substances that some individuals may be sensitive or allergic to.

The following is excerpted from the Essene Gospel of John as translated by Edward Szekely.

"Let the angels of God prepare your bread. Moisten your wheat, that the angels of water may enter it. Then set it in the air, that the angel of air may embrace it. And leave it from morning to evening beneath the sun, that the angel of sunshine may descend upon it. And the blessings of the three angels will soon make the germ of life to sprout in your wheat. Then crush your grain, and make thin wafers, as did your forefathers when they departed out of Egypt, the house of bondage. Put them back again beneath the sun from its appearing, and when it is risen to its highest in the heavens, turn them over on the other side that they may be embraced there also by the angel of sunshine, and leave them there until the sun sets. For the angels of water, and air and of sunshine fed and ripened the wheat in the field, and they likewise must prepare also your bread. And the same sun which, with the fire of life, made the wheat to grow and ripen, must cook your bread with the same fire. For the fire of the sun gives life to the wheat, to the bread, and to the body. But the fire of death kills the wheat, the bread, and the body. And the living angels of the living God serve only living men. For God is the God of the living, and not the God of the dead. "

Of all the known breads, the simplest and the most nutritious is Essene bread. The only difference between the baking technique used by the monastic brotherhood 2,000+ years ago and our modern method is that they baked their bread in the sun while we use an oven. Both methods create in a round, flattened loaf—rather like a sweet, moist dessert bread or cake—containing all of the virtues of unadulterated sprouted grain . . . its sole ingredient.

Making Essene Bread

Begin by making wheat sprouts. Measure the desired amount of wheat berries and use the directions for sprouting from the text above. After the grain has sprouted, grind the sprouted wheat berries into a paste.

Before handling the dough, wet your hands to minimize stickiness. Work the dough briefly to get out any air pockets, and then shape it into circular, somewhat flattened loaves. Place them on an oiled cookie sheet and bake them at low temperature (about 180-200 degrees F) (80-90 degrees C). It is done when you can press on the bottom of it and it springs back. This may take about two hours depending on your oven temperature and the humidity. For best results, make the loaves very thin. The inside will be quite soft, developing a firmer texture upon cooling. It is chewy, tasty, and very nutritious. It is very moist and chewy compared to conventional bread.

To make an even tastier version, add some raisins, dates, figs, other dried fruits and nuts.

If you live in a place and time that has abundant hot sunshine, I encourage you to experiment with baking the Essene bread in the sun according to the ancient tradition. If you own a solar oven, you can do this most anytime, even in partially overcast conditions. Some believe that bread so prepared possesses extra vitality.

Stir-Fried Sprouts

Heat a tablespoon of oil or butter in a wok or heavy frying pan. To this add the following ingredients:

2 cups wheat sprouts
2 cups legume sprouts
1 onion, chopped, or dried onion flakes
1 cup chopped carrots (parsnips, turnips, beets, celeriac, kohlrabi or other root vegetable)
1 cup shredded Kale (cabbage, mustard greens, spinach)
1 tbs. soy sauce

Sauté these ingredients for about five minutes.

Hash Browned Potatoes and Sprouts

Precook 3 large potatoes by baking or boiling them with the jackets on. Dice the potatoes and add these ingredients:

Diced Potatoes
2 tbs. oil or butter
1 cup wheat sprouts
1 cup bean sprouts
1 tsp salt
1 tsp garlic powder

Sauté these ingredients for 3 to 5 minutes.

Mushrooms and Sprouts

1 cup alfalfa (or bean) sprouts
1 cup wheat sprouts
2 tbs. oil or butter
1/2 cup chopped onion
1/2 cup diced celery (fennel, or parsley)
1 cup sliced mushrooms
soy sauce to taste

Sauté these ingredients for about five minutes.

Kale, Greens and Sprouts

Combine the following ingredients:

1 cup bean, pea, or lentil sprouts
1 cup wheat sprouts
2 tbs. oil or butter
2 cup shredded Kale
1/2 tsp garlic powder
1 tbs. soy sauce

Sauté these ingredients for about 5 minutes. You can substitute other greens for the Kale.

Sprout Burgers

Combine the following ingredients:

4 cups wheat sprouts
1 cup bean sprouts (mung, adzuki, etc.)
1 cup soybean sprouts
1 cup lentil or pea sprouts
1 onion, diced
1 clove garlic
2 eggs, beaten
1 cup milk
4 tbs. wheat flour
salt and pepper to taste

Mix all of these ingredients and form them into patties. Broil or fry them until they are brown. This patty resembles egg foo young.

Wheat Sprout Salad

Combine the following ingredients:
Recipe 1:

Combine the following ingredients:

3 cups wheat sprouts
1 cup bean sprouts
1 cup finely chopped parsley (or celery)
1 onion, diced (or 6-8 green onions)
2 cucumbers, peeled and diced
2 tomatoes, diced
1/4 cup olive oil
Juice of one lemon
1 tsp garlic powder
salt and pepper to taste

Sautee the wheat and bean sprouts lightly, let them cool, them mix with the other ingredients and let them marinate for several hours. Serve this dish cold.

Recipe 2:

Combine the following ingredients:

3 cups fresh Wheat Sprouts (or any grain sprouts)
1 cup grated carrots (or beets, turnips, radishes, etc.)
3/4 cup minced Onion
3 tbs. olive, coconut, peanut oil or butter
1 1/2 tbs. fresh Lemon Juice (or apple cider or balsamic vinegar)

Sprinkle with paprika or pepper. Serve on bed of lettuce (or other salad greens) or lightly sauteed greens (wildcrafted edible weeds or garden greens).

Recipe 3:

Combine the following ingredients:

2 cups sprouted wheat berries
3 tablespoons red wine vinegar (or other vinegar)
3/4 teaspoons salt
1/2 teaspoon fresh crushed pepper
3 tbs olive, coconut, peanut oil or butter
1 medium red onion julienne (or other onion or scallion)
1/2 cup chopped dill
1/4 cup chopped cilantro

Blend the red wine vinegar, salt, and pepper in a bowl. Slowly add the oil in a slow steady stream to create an emulsion. In another bowl, toss the sprouted wheat berries, onions, and herbs together. Add the dressing.

You can also add tomatoes, raisins, dried apricots, walnuts, pecans, pine nuts or other nuts, chopped apples, or pears.

Creamed Sprouts

Combine the following ingredients:

2 cup wheat sprouts

Saute or steam the sprouts for about 5 minutes then add:

2 tbs. butter or oil
2 tbs. flour
1 cup milk
salt and pepper to taste

Mix the milk, butter, and oil first. Then bring them to a simmer, add the other ingredients, and cook them for about 5 minutes.

Hot Cooked Sprout Cereal

Combine the following ingredients:

4 cups fresh sprouted wheat
salt to taste
honey to taste
milk

Cook the sprouts for a few minutes or until they are soft.

Recipe 2:

Combine the following ingredients:

1 cup wheat sprouts
1 tsp butter
1/4 cup raisins, prunes or other dried fruits
salt to taste

Place this mixture in a sauce pan and cover it with water. Simmer until it is cooked. Add water as needed. Serve this with milk and honey.

Sprout Cereals

Sprouts made from any of the grains can be eaten raw as a cold cereal. Wheat and buckwheat are top choices. Just add milk, your choices of available fresh or dried fruits, berries and nuts.

If you like a hot cereal, you can cook sprouts by boiling or steaming. The wheat / rye family of denser grains work best for cooking. Buckwheat is softer and quickly becomes mushy, so cook it lightly

Sprout Fish Chowder

2 1/2 cup hot water
1-2 (6 1/2-oz) cans tuna
3 tbsp butter
1 cup wheat sprouts
1/2 cup chopped onion
1/2 cup canned or cooked peas
1/2 cup chopped celery
1/2 cup shredded carrots (or salsify, parsnips, beets or potatoes)

Put all of the ingredients into a saucepan and bring them to a boil. Lower the heat to medium and cook for 15 minutes. Blend the following and add to the hot mixture:

2 cup hot water
3/4 cup dry milk powder
1 1/2 tsp salt
1/4 cup cornstarch (or freshly ground flour)
1/8 tsp pepper

Heat this to just below boiling and stir until thickened.

Important Point

You can eat sprouts raw. That means that you don't have to spend time and fuel cooking. Sprout salads or sprouts eaten as a cereal is one way to do this. Munching on wheat sprouts as a snack is also good.

Sourdough

In the most ancient of times, flat bread was made from ground grains and water. One day someone allowed water and flour mash to sit on the shelf too long and it fermented. Disgusted but still hungry, this desperate soul cooked it anyway and discovered sourdough bread. The dough is soured by yeast and bacteria that causes the formation of carbon dioxide bubbles which cause the dough to rise and form lighter, spongier bread.

Sourdough baking has an origin somewhere prior to recorded history. Until the 1800's, sourdough was the only way to bake bread. Today, it is uncommon but still used. Using sourdough techniques is a direct substitute for using commercial yeast to make your bread rise. There are sourdough cultures in use that have been perpetuated for hundreds and perhaps thousands of years. All of these cultures originated from wild yeast and bacteria combinations somewhere.

When you are making sourdough don't forget that the dough has to be warm to rise. One of the most common mistakes is to allow insufficient time or temperature for rising. Sourdough is usually slower to rise than commercial yeast. Different cultures have a different speed. Some of them require 24 hours for the bread to rise properly.

Sourdough is bread that has been leavened with a wild yeast culture. The culture is maintained in a dough sample which becomes 'sour' due to the action of the yeast and bacteria. A dough sample is then inoculated with the dough starter and allowed to rise.

Many people like the taste of sourdough bread. The characteristic flavor of sourdough bread is due to the lactobacillus bacteria rather than the yeast which causes the bread to rise. The bacteria take longer, about 24 hours, to produce the flavor while modern bakers yeast will rise the bread in approximately 2 hours. Therefore, to get the flavor, use a traditional or freshly developed culture and give it plenty of time to develop.

In addition to flavor, the bacteria create a variety of anti-biotics and an acid medium which inhibit spoilage organisms. Therefore, sourdough bread will keep better and last longer on the shelf than regular bread with the same ingredients and in the same environment.

Capturing a Sourdough Culture

You can capture a culture from the air. Combine 2 cups of flour and 2 cups of warm water in a bowl and sit it in the open to collect the microorganisms from the air. Stir the mixture vigorously once every 24 hours. In 2 to 3 days, bubbles should appear on the surface. Add an additional cup of flour and water and stir. Repeat the feeding at approximately 12 hour intervals for several days. When the captured culture is active enough to be useful, it will form a layer of foam on the surface that is 1 to 2 inches deep. If it has not achieved this level of activity within 4 to 5 days, you should probably toss it and start over.

A related method is to mix grapes or berries with the flour and water mixture. The fruits generally have yeasts and bacteria present on their surface. It is important to use wildcrafted fruits or organically grown fruits to avoid the impact of pesticides, fungicides and antibiotics that may have been sprayed on commercial fruits.

Getting a good culture requires both active yeast and a compatible strain of lactobacillus bacteria. This may require some trial and error experimentation to get a starter with the right characteristics and flavor.

Activating a Sourdough Culture

If you purchase a commercial sourdough starter, it may have been dried or freeze dried to preserve it. Whether fresh or preserved, it will need to be activated and fed to make it productive.

Add the culture to 1 cup of flour and ¾ cup of warm water. Let this mixture set for about 12 hours at 85 to 90 degrees F (29-32 degrees C). Add another cup of flour and ¾ cup of warm water and let it sit for another 12 hours. If the culture hasn't bubbled up and shown itself to be satisfactorily active, discard half of it, add another cup of flour and ¾ cup of warm water and let it set for another 12 hours. Repeat again if necessary. Some cultures will fully activate in 1-2 days while others may take 3-7 days.

Starter stored in a refrigerator should be fed every two weeks. Do not freeze a starter. For long term storage, dry a fresh starter. After drying thoroughly, it can be placed in the freezer.

Before using this to activate the dough for your bread, separate out one cup of this mixture, add a cup of flour and ¾ cup of warm water to it and place it in the refrigerator to start the next batch.

A Baker's Yeast Culture

Commercial baker's yeast is quite different from a sourdough culture. Baker's yeast is far more active and will cause bread to rise much faster than wild yeast. Sourdough cultures made from wild yeast vary widely in their activity and in the flavor imparted to the bread.

To create a baker's yeast based sourdough starter, do the following:

To a non-metallic (stainless steel is OK) container with a lid add:

2 cups warm water
2 cups fresh whole wheat flour
1 package dry yeast

Place this mixture in a warm place and allow it to rise overnight. Now you have a sourdough starter. You have to keep renewing it as you use it.

This culture will make the bread rise, but it will be faster than a wild culture and may not contain the bacteria necessary to impart the characteristic sourdough flavor.

Milk Based Sourdough Starter

Using milk or yogurt with a live culture will introduce lactobacillus bacteria into the mixture.

Recipe 1:

2 cups buttermilk or yogurt with live culture
2 cups flour
1 packet yeast

Allow this mixture to set for two days before using it.

In this starter you have the yeast fermenting the flour and the lactobacillus bacteria fermenting the milk sugars.

Recipe 2:

2 cups flour
2 cups milk
1 tbs. yeast
2 tbs. honey
A small amount of live lactobacillus culture from buttermilk, kefir or yogurt.

Allow this mixture to set for two days before using it. Use this batter in the recipes described below for a more strongly flavored sourdough.

While using dairy products and commercial yeast may not equal a developed sourdough culture, they can be used if you don't have one. However, the lactobacillus bacteria in yogurt and buttermilk are adapted to metabolizing milk sugars rather than grain starches. Therefore, you will need to use milk in the recipes.

Sourdough Batter

To make a basic sourdough batter, place the following ingredients in a non-metallic container and allow it to set in a warm place overnight:

1 cup sourdough starter
2 cups warm water
2 cups fresh flour

SPONGE ?

Sources for Sourdough Starter

Here are a few sources of good established sourdough starters.

Oregon Trail Sourdough
P. O. Box 321
Jefferson, MD 21755 USA
http://carlsfriends.net/source.html

Sourdoughs International
PO Box 670
Cascade, Idaho   83611
208-382-4828
http://sourdo.com/culture.htm

This is an excellent source for some great sourdough starters.

Use your favorite search engine to locate more.

Cooking Grains and Legumes

Cooking Wheat

This applies to the other hard grains as well including spelt, kamut, rye, triticale, oat groats and barley. To cook wheat, blow the chaff out of it, rinse it, cover it with water, soak it overnight, and boil it until the grain swells and becomes soft. It is better if you soak it first and even better if you allow the grains to sprout. Sprouting converts the starches to sugar and dramatically increases the vitamin content of the grain. The sprouts need be only 1/8 to 1/4 inches long to give you the big nutritional boost of extra vitamin content.

You can eat the sprouted wheat raw without cooking. The texture isn't much different than cooked wheat. Except for the sweetness added by the sprouting, there is no distinguishable difference between cooked wheat and cooked sprouted wheat.

And of course, you may want to add a small amount of salt to the gruel. Gruel is a term usually used to describe cooked cereal grains. What you have then is something that is quite chewy, slightly nutty in flavor, and nutritious. It makes a superior substitute for breakfast cereals. It can get boring if you eat it too often of course. Fortunately, it is very versatile and you can do many creative things with it.

Another approach is to take some clean wheat kernels (also called wheat berries) and boil them until they swell and become soft. This cooking process works even better if you crack the wheat first. To crack wheat, simply set the burrs of your wheat grinder to a wide gap and run some wheat through it. Instead of fine flour, you will get cracked wheat and a small amount of the fine starch from the kernels.

I recommend the use of a stainless steel pressure cooker. With one of these fine instruments, you simply pour wheat into the pot to a depth of about one inch and add water to stand about one inch above the wheat. Bring the pressure cooker up to a jiggle, take it off of the fire and let it cool down and de-pressurize. By the time it is de-pressurized, the wheat will be finished. You can enhance this process by sitting the hot pot in a box filled with insulating material. The insulating material can be a blanket, styrofoam beads, etc. The insulation holds the heat in and increases the cooking time without using any more fuel.

Cooked wheat prepared in this way can be used as a direct substitute for rice in any dish. The taste and texture are different from rice. It is chewier and has a somewhat nutty flavor.

Bulgur

Bulgur is precooked, dried, cracked wheat. It is toasted in appearance, nutty in flavor, and easily adaptable to favorite dishes. Bulgur has the advantage of cooking more rapidly than whole or cracked wheat. It is humanity's oldest processed food. The Bible calls it "parched corn". You may know it as an ingredient of tabouli, but this is a whole wheat version that has more flavor and nutrition than store bought.

How to Make Bulgur

- Place the wheat in a pot and add about twice as much water as there is wheat. Bring it to a boil and cook for about 1 hour, or until the wheat kernels are tender and swollen.

- Drain the liquid from the wheat and place the cooked wheat on trays in a dehydrator, or spread it on baking sheets for oven drying. Dehydrate it until it is completely dry. If using an oven, set it for about 175 degrees F (80 degrees C) and stir it frequently.

- Use a grain mill or food processor to crack the wheat. Use a course setting so the wheat is cracked rather than ground into flour. Store it in an air-tight container until ready to cook. Prepared bulgur can be used in salads like tabouli, cooked as a pilaf, or used in place of rice in casseroles.

Bulgur Salad

Bulgur is cracked wheat that has been cooked and then dried.

Combine the following ingredients:

3 cups dry wheat bulgur
2 cloves fresh crushed garlic
(other herbs such as cilantro, parsley, or dill)
1/4 cup olive oil
Juice of two lemons or apple cider vinegar
Enough liquid to hydrate the dried bulgur
1 cup cooked garbanzo or kidney beans
1 cucumber, sliced
1 tomato, sliced
salt to taste

Allow to soak for about four hours.

Feel free to add other salad vegetables, other types of legumes, and other herbs and spices to taste.

Tabouli Salad

Combine the following ingredients:

1/2 cups bulgur
2 cups cold water
3 medium tomatoes, diced
1/2 cups parsley, chopped
1/4 cups chopped green onions
2 tbsp fresh mint, chopped
2 tbsp oil (olive)
2 tbsp lemon juice
1 tsp salt
1/4 tsp pepper

In large bowl, stir the bulgur with water; let it stand 1 1/2 hours until the bulgur softens and rehydrates. Drain the bulgur well. Add the tomatoes and remaining ingredients and mix well. Cover and chill for at least 1 hour.

Bulgur Minestrone Soup

Place in a pan with a small amount of water the following ingredients:

3/4 cup chopped onions
1 cup chopped celery

Stir fry or steam these ingredients until the celery starts to soften then add:

1 cup bulgur
1/4 tsp pepper
1 cup shredded cabbage
1/4 tsp oregano
1/2 cup cooked kidney beans
1/2 tsp salt
1/2 cup sliced carrots
1 1/2 quarts water
1 cup green beans or peas
1/2 cup minced parsley
1 cup sliced zucchini

If you lack any ingredients, either delete that ingredient or substitute another. You can substitute miso or soy sauce for salt and you can delete the salt and cabbage and substitute a cup of home made sauerkraut. Canned or dried vegetables work nicely too. Dried tomatoes or tomato powder add flavor to any soup. Simmer this brew for 15 to 20 minutes then serve it with fresh crackers and cheese.

Bulgur Bullion and Gravy

Grind dried bulgur in your wheat mill. Add the powder to boiling water to obtain the desired consistency. Add miso or soy sauce to obtain the right saltiness.

Popped and Parched Wheat

LESS FAT KIND

Parched wheat can be made by heating an iron skillet with a little coconut oil and adding a small quantity of wheat. You can try this with other grains too. Some of it may pop, but not as well as popcorn. The resulting roasted or parched seed will be tender enough to eat directly or to easily grind into meal. You have seen parched corn in the form of corn nuts. Eat it as a snack or as a cereal. Ground parched barley is called tsampa.

Popcorn pops because the moisture inside the kernel gets heated into steam and the pressure causes the outer hull to explode. To make something similar happen to wheat, it needs to have higher moisture content. Different wheat varieties will perform differently and it won't be like popcorn. To pop wheat:

- Soak the grain for 12 hours.
- Cook the grain for about 30 minutes.   *How?*
- Drain and dry the grain.
- Heat an iron skillet with a bit of coconut oil.
- Add the wheat berries and cover.

In my experience, very few of the wheat grains actually pop. This is probably because of the kind of wheat that I use. It mostly ends up as parched wheat. It is crunchy and has a delicious nutty flavor. Be careful to not overcook it.

How to Cook Beans

Start with dried beans. This applies to all of the dried beans including pinto beans, kidney beans, black beans, garbanzo beans, lima beans, etc. Lentils and split peas do not take as long to cook. At night, wash and sort out any bad beans or pebbles and cover with water. Dried beans will swell to twice their dried size, so cover with plenty of water. In the morning, drain and wash beans. I like to give them a little extra time both soaking and sitting after they have soaked so that the sprouting process can start. You don't

73

want it to go too far, just the slightest indication that it has begun. The sprouts of many beans taste awful, but the minimal sprouting activates enzymes that partially break down the stuff that causes gas.

The preferred cooking utensil is a stainless steel pressure pot. Bring the pot up to a jiggle and turn down the heat to just keep it pressurized for about 5 to 10 minutes. Then turn off the heat and let it cool down. By the time the pressure releases, the beans will be well done.

Alternatively, you can use a regular cooking pot and let the beans simmer for 4 to 6 hours. Another alternative is to use a crock pot for a similar time.

The flavor is enhanced if you add a bit of meat or meat bones to the pot.

Baking Bread

Grinding Wheat into Flour

I have emphasized sprouting for its nutritional benefits. Nevertheless, most bread and other baked goods are made from whole wheat flour rather than sprouted wheat dough. It takes 3 to 5 days to sprout a batch of wheat berries, so you have to plan in advance. Use the sprout approach as much as possible.

If you had to live on a strict diet of wheat the sprouting would be absolutely necessary. Your health and your life would depend on it. If you are able to enjoy a varied diet that also includes fresh vegetables and fruits, you can enjoy the convenience, variety, and texture of foods made from whole wheat flour. You can also make bread from sprouted wheat just as well as from unsprouted wheat.

Grinding wheat into flour is an essential part of utilizing wheat as a food. The grinding breaks the grains down into small particles to make them more digestible.

Whole grain wheat that is kept DRY and COOL can be stored for a very long time. If you have any doubts about the quality of stored grain, sprout a batch of it. If it sprouts, it is alive. Because it is alive, the essential oils in the germ do not go rancid. The bran around the kernel provides a protective surface which keeps out mold and bacteria.

Grinding the wheat into flour crushes the bran, germ, and starches into a fine dust which is easier to cook and digest. Of course the wheat is no longer alive and is now subject to mold, decay, and loss of nutritional value. Freshly ground flour should be used within a few days if unrefrigerated and within about 2 weeks if refrigerated.

Commercial white flour has the bran and germ removed so that it will have a much greater shelf life. This process also removes the essential oils, B vitamins, and much of the fiber from the flour. Enriched flour has synthetically replaced 5 of the 35 natural ingredients that were removed by the milling and bleaching process. Freshly ground whole wheat flour and foodstuffs made from it will spoil quickly because they contain the essential ingredients to support life.

If it doesn't spoil quickly, that means that molds, fungus and bacteria don't consider it edible. If the mold, bacteria, insects and mice don't eat it, should you? Incidentally, there is also a tremendous difference in flavor. Guess which one is better.

In ancient times people ground their seeds and grains between two rocks. In some parts of the world, this is still common. It works, but it is a lot of time consuming work. A modern hand cranked grain mill is much more efficient. To live on wheat and other grains means having your own grinder or mill. There are several good hand cranked and electric models on the market. The better ones tend to be a bit expensive but will last a lifetime if reasonably cared for.

Turning the mill by hand to get a quantity of flour for a big user is time consuming. Most people who try this approach get bored standing in front of their mill for all of the hours that it requires to feed their family. Some of the hand powered models can be readily adapted to a motor by means of a pulley and belt. It is most prudent to own a quality mill that can be hand driven, just in case. Some of the electric models have optional hand cranks for emergency use. When using a motor, gear it to turn the mill slowly to avoid excess heat. Heat will damage the essential oils in the germ.

Traditionally, the finest flours have been produced by stone burrs. Now, the higher quality metal burrs are able to produce flour equal to stone burrs. Stone burrs, however, cannot be used to grind wet or oily material since it clogs the stones. There are several mills on the market that use high speed impellers to shatter the grain. These work well but are not adaptable to manual operation. If you choose one of these, you should have a spare mill that can be operated by hand for emergencies.

Notes on Baking Bread

The first thing to consider is that your flour and the bread made from it will have different characteristics than commercial products.

- Your grain and the flour made from it will have a different moisture content than commercial products. Your moisture content will be unknown while the commercial product will be standardized.

- Your grain and the flour made from it will have a different protein content than commercial products. Your protein content may be higher or lower than the standardized product. The gluten portion of the protein may also vary resulting in different rising characteristics between different varieties of wheat.

- The gluten in your flour will be fresh rather than bleached or aged so it may not rise as well.

- Your flour will contain more fiber (bran) than the commercial product and this will affect texture.

- Your flour will contain the natural oils from the germ and will, therefore, be more perishable and more nutritious.

- Strongly chlorinated water or naturally alkaline water may inhibit the yeast and interfere with bread rising.

- Salt is not an essential ingredient, but it does stabilize yeast fermentation and stiffen the gluten.

- Fats and oils may increase loaf volume, prevent crust cracking, enhance keeping qualities and improving slicing qualities.

- Sugar or sweeteners may be used in small amounts to feed the yeast and accelerate their growth.

Many of the recipes call for a "**legume protein complement**". The purpose of this is to complement the grain protein and make the protein more assimilable. Complementary proteins may include:

- Soybean flour. Make certain that it has been heat processed.

- Peanut flour.

- Sweet lupine flour.

- TVP (textured vegetable protein) that has been ground in your grain grinder.

- Cooked beans or peas or dehydrated cooked beans or peas. (never uncooked)

The Art of Bread Making

After you have read a few cookbooks, you get the idea that the basic recipes are all pretty much the same. They all strive to be unique and superior by varying the subtle factors, like small differences in ingredients or preparation methods. Anyone can make good whole wheat bread. Making great whole wheat bread may require a little practice and some fiddling with the subtle factors.

With whole wheat bread, there is one variable that will always require a bit of fine tuning of the recipe. That variable is the flour. Its two variables are the protein content of the wheat that you use and the coarseness of your grind. The coarseness of the grind is controlled by you, the quality of your mill, and how you have it adjusted. The protein content is determined by how carefully you shopped for your wheat supply.

Always sift your flour before mixing the ingredients. Sifting breaks up any lumps that would impede effective mixing. You can also separate out part of the bran and coarse ground particles of wheat. Separating them out will make the flour rise more and you can sprinkle them onto the crust before baking.

You will have to adjust the liquid content of some recipes slightly to account for this unpredictable variable. Getting the liquid content correct means the difference between bread that is too moist, not moist enough, or perhaps even hard or crumbly. You know that the liquid content is correct when the dough that you are kneading does not stick to the sides of the pan or to your fingers. If it is sticky, add a little more dry flour. If it is too dry to incorporate all of the flour, add a little liquid, but only a tiny amount.

Another important factor is kneading. This forms the gluten molecules and enables the bread to rise properly. You will probably have to knead the bread for 5 to 15 minutes. Kneading means squeezing, stretching, rolling, and twisting the dough mass. It has been kneaded adequately when you can stick your finger in it and the depression bounces back.

Rising the bread is the next important element. The rising is caused by the carbon dioxide given off by the yeast. The yeast is introduced by the commercial dry yeast that you add, or from the sourdough starter that you add to the flour, water, and other ingredients. Adequate rising requires a warm place. In cold weather, I turn the oven on just long enough to get it warm, turn it off, and then place the bread inside. Mixing a little sweetener with the dough gives the yeast some extra food and enables them to act more quickly. Any sweetener will feed the yeast.

If you lack sweetener, you can make your own. Malt is simply a sugar produced from sprouted grain.

Making Malt

To make malt:

- Sprout one cup of wheat berries
- Dry the sprouts thoroughly
- Grind them to a powder

Add it to any of the bread recipes at the rate of 1/4 tsp for each loaf of bread. If a recipe calls for honey or sugar, you may substitute malt.

Most recipes call for allowing the dough to double in height, and then bake it. If it rises much higher, it may develop bubbles. A higher rise may make lighter bread, but you may need to add eggs, milk, etc. to increase the cohesiveness. Many whole wheat bread recipes use commercial unbleached or white flour to improve the texture of the bread. When you are relying on your own fresh grind, you can't do that. After you have practiced a little, you will also realize that it is quite unnecessary.

The other method of making bread rise is to use baking powder or baking soda. This substance gives off carbon dioxide gas when heated. This method is used in pancakes, pan breads, etc. One trick that can be used is to add baking soda to sourdough batter. The reaction of the acids in the sourdough with the soda gives off carbon dioxide gas and causes immediate rising. You have to be quick however. <u>For health considerations, avoid baking powders that contain aluminum compounds.</u>

Sprouted Wheat Bread

In addition to Essene bread, sprouted wheat can also be used for more traditional leavened bread. Yeast, either from bakery supplies or your sourdough starter are very happy to eat the sugars produced by the sprouting of the wheat and produce gas bubbles to make the bread rise.

Recipe 1:

Combine the following ingredients:

5 cups sprouted and ground wheat paste
1 cup Legume Protein Complement
1 tbs. yeast
1 tsp salt

Mix these ingredients into stiff dough adding a small amount of dry flour to absorb some of the excess liquid if necessary. How much you add will depend on the moisture content in the sprout dough. Keep adding dry flour a little at a time until the dough loses most of its stickiness. Knead thoroughly and allow it to rise to about twice the original size. Kneading the dough for a longer period of time will also reduce the stickiness and minimize the amount of dry flour that you will need. Bake this dough at 300 degrees F (150 degrees C) for about 45 minutes or until done.

It is done when you can press on the top and bottom and it springs back. This bread will be more moist and chewy than normal bread but not as moist or flat as Essene bread. It will also be delicious. You can add more honey and dried fruits, nuts, and spices to add new flavors. Don't be shy about experimenting.

As a variation, add 1 cup whole soaked raisins and 1 cup of shredded carrots.

Recipe 2:

Combine the following ingredients:

4 cups dried and ground wheat sprouts
3 cups whole wheat flour
1 cup Legume Protein Complement
1 tbs. salt

Dissolve 2 envelopes of dry yeast and 1/4 cup of honey in 3 cups of warm water. Gradually mix in the dry ingredients and 3 tbs. of cooking oil. Beat until the mixture can be kneaded then knead for about 10 to 15 minutes until dough is smooth and stretchy. Let this dough rise in warm place until it doubles in bulk. Divide this dough into two loaves and let it rise again until it doubles in bulk. Bake this dough at 350 degrees F (177 degrees C) for about 45 minutes or until done.

Sprouted Wheat Sourdough Bread

Combine the following ingredients:

3 cups ground wheat sprouts
1 cup Legume Protein Complement
2 cup sourdough batter
1 tsp salt

Knead this mixture into stiff dough and allow it to rise to twice its original height. If needed, add a little dry flour to form stiff dough that does not stick to the pan. Bake this dough in a 300 degree F (150 degree C) oven for about 45 minutes or until done.

Sprouted Wheat Biscuits

Combine the following ingredients:

2 cups ground wheat sprouts
1 cup wheat flour
1/2 cup Legume Protein Complement
5 tsp baking powder
1/2 tsp salt
2 tbs. oil or butter
enough milk (or water) to form dough balls

Form this mixture into dough balls and place them on an oiled baking sheet. Bake them at 450 degrees for about 15 minutes.

Wheat Sprout Pancakes

Combine the following ingredients:

1 cup wheat sprouts
3 tbs oil or butter
1 cup whole wheat flour
1 cup milk
1/2 tsp salt
2 eggs
2 tbs honey
1 tsp baking powder
1/4 cup Legume Protein Complement

Mix these ingredients into a batter and spoon it into a hot iron skillet with a little olive or coconut oil.

Sourdough Pancakes

Recipe 1:

To make sourdough pancakes use any of the basic batters or starters described above and treat them as pancake batter. You can add a small amount of flour if you want to make a thicker pancake.

Recipe 2:

To the basic batter, add a tbs. of baking soda. Mix and fold it in quickly. The batter is acid and the baking soda is alkaline. The resulting reaction releases a lot of carbon dioxide bubbles that makes a bubbly, fluffy, batter. Mix in the baking soda just before you spoon it into the skillet. In contrast, the basic batter will produce a relatively flat and thin pancake that is also quite delicious.

Recipe 3:

Combine and mix the following ingredients:

4 cups of basic batter
1 (or 2) eggs
1 tsp baking powder (or soda)
2 tbs oil
1 tsp salt
1 tbs honey
1/4 cup of milk

You can also toss in blueberries, blackberries, nuts, and other goodies if available. Other types of flours can be blended including cornmeal, amaranth, rye, triticale, and millet.

Sourdough Biscuits

Recipe 1:

Mix and knead together the following ingredients:

1 cup sourdough batter
2 cups whole wheat flour
2 tsp baking powder
1/2 cup Legume Protein Complement
2 tbs honey
2 tbs salt
Enough water to make stiff dough

Knead the dough and roll it into a long round mass. Cut one half inch pieces off with an oiled knife and place them on an oiled cookie sheet. Allow them to rise to about twice their original thickness. Bake them at 300 degrees F (150 degrees C) or until done.

Recipe 2:

Gently mix and knead together the following ingredients:

1/2 cup sourdough batter
2 tbs yellow cornmeal
1 cups fresh whole wheat flour
1/4 cup Legume Protein Complement
1 cup milk

Allow this mixture to sit in a warm covered non-metallic container overnight. Then add:

1/2 tsp salt
1 1/2 cup fresh flour
2 tbs. honey
2 tsp baking powder

Mix and knead this mixture until the dough is stiff enough to not stick to the sides of the pan. Knead this dough about 10 to 12 times then allow it to sit for about ten minutes. Roll the dough into a 1/2 inch thick sheet and cut it into squares with a knife. Oil the blade of the knife to prevent sticking. Oil the surface of the biscuits and place in an oiled pan. Allow the biscuits to rise to about 1 inch high then bake them in a 375 degree F (190 degrees C) oven until they are browned.

Simple Sourdough Bread

The simplest sourdough bread is made with only wheat, water, and sourdough starter. To make this simple bread, mix the following ingredients:

2 cups whole wheat flour
1 cup sourdough batter
1/4 cup Legume Protein Complement
Enough liquid to form smooth dough
1 tsp salt (optional)

Knead this dough thoroughly and let it rise to about twice its original height. Bake this bread dough at 350 degrees F (177 degrees C) for about 45 minutes or until done.

Basic Sourdough Bread

The next simplest sourdough bread is made with only a few more ingredients.

Place in a non-metallic bowl the following ingredients:

2 cups sourdough batter
4 cups fresh flour
2 tbs honey
2 tbs oil
1 tsp salt
1/2 cup Legume Protein Complement

Knead this dough for about ten minutes and place it in an oiled loaf pan. Allow it to rise to about twice the size of the original dough then bake it at 350 degrees F (177 degrees C) for about forty five minutes or until it is done. You can use milk instead of water and you can add a couple of eggs to the batter to richen it up a bit. You can also add raisins, prunes, or figs as well as nuts with wonderful results.

Flat Bread and Tortillas

The simplest and one of the most ancient of breads is flat bread. It is simply an unleavened pancake like bread made from wheat and water and a little salt. The tortilla is one of the versions of this type of bread.

Recipe

Mix together the following ingredients:

2 1/2 cups fresh wheat flour
1/2 cup Legume Protein Complement
1 tsp salt
1 cup water to make stiff dough
1 tbs baking powder (optional)

Knead this dough for a few minutes and divide it into baseball sized balls and roll each one into a flat round pancake approximately 1/16 inch thick. Place it onto a hot oiled iron skillet or griddle and cook it on each side for a few minutes. Use it as a flour tortilla.

The other option is to take the pancake and cut it into 1/4 to 1/2 inch strips with a sharp knife. These noodles can be added to soups or boiled in water as a side dish.

The baking powder will make the tortillas or noodles lighter but good results will be obtained without it as well.

Pita Bread

Mix together the following ingredients:

2 cups flour
1 tbsp active dry yeast
1 1/4 cup hot water
1/2 tsp salt

Gradually add another 2 cups flour until dough clings to the sides of bowl. The dough should be moderately stiff. Knead the dough about 5 minutes until it is smooth and elastic. Form the dough into 10 balls. On a floured counter top, roll each ball from the center out, into a 1/4-inch thick and 6 inches round shape. Make sure both sides are covered with flour. Place it on a lightweight, nonstick baking sheet. Let it rise 30 minutes or until it is slightly raised. Preheat oven to 500 degrees F (260 degrees C). Gently turn the rounds upside down just before placing them in the oven. Bake on the bottom rack of the oven. The instant hot heat makes the breads puff up.

Simple Whole Wheat Bread

The simplest bread is made from whole wheat flour, water, and a leavening agent. To make this simple bread, combine the following ingredients:

2 cups fresh whole wheat flour
1/2 cup Legume Protein Complement
3/4 cup water
1 tbs yeast

Mix the dry ingredients thoroughly, then add the water and form into a dough ball. Knead the dough until it is firm and elastic, about 5 to 10 minutes. Place it in a warm place and allow it to rise to about twice its original size. Bake it for about 45 minutes at 300 degrees F (150 degrees C) or until done.

This bread turns out surprisingly good. The flavor is very good, better than supermarket fare in my opinion. The flavor is enhanced, however, by adding a little salt and honey to the mixture. The texture is good but it is much denser than supermarket fare. This is not a problem, you just have to adjust to the fact that there is a lot more nutrition packed into each slice than what you are accustomed to.

It is good to know that you can make bread even if you had only wheat and water to work with. If you didn't have yeast for leavening, you can use sourdough starter instead.

Basic Whole Wheat Bread

Make a yeast mixture by adding 2 tbs of dry yeast and 1 tbs honey or sugar to 1/2 cup of warm water and allowing it to stand for 10 minutes.

Place the following ingredients into a non-metallic bowl (stainless steel is OK):

9 cups fresh flour
1 cup Legume Protein Complement
1 tbs salt
2 cups powdered milk

Add to this mixture:

2 cups warm water
yeast mixture
1/4 cup honey
1/4 cup oil

Mix thoroughly then continue to knead this dough for about 10 minutes. Separate the dough into three loaves and place them into a greased pan. Allow the loaves to rise to about twice their original size then bake them at 300 degrees F (150 degrees C) for about 45 minutes or until done.

The kneading process is important. Squeeze and stretch the dough in long flowing movements rather than short hard ones. The kneaded dough should be elastic when you finish with it. If you bake a lot of bread, a kitchen aid with a dough hook or something equivalent is a real asset to enhance the kneading effort.

Pizza Crust

Any of the bread dough recipes will make a good pizza crust. Roll it <u>VERY</u> thin, place it in a greased pizza pan and allow it to rise. You can use a pie pan to make a deep dish pizza. Put the sauce and pizza stuff on top and bake it. Do this and commercial pizza crusts will taste like cardboard forever more.

Dried Bread

Bread made from fresh whole wheat flour tends to mold and spoil fairly quickly compared to commercial breads. This is because it contains more nutrients and no chemicals intended to inhibit life processes. To extend its shelf life and to create a lightweight trail food, dry some of it. To dry it, cut it into thin slices and put them in a dryer, on a sunny window sill, or in an oven set to low. Dried bread can be eaten straight, added to soups, or steamed. Removing all water makes it difficult for bacteria and mold to grow. Dried bread has been referred to as "hardtack" and other names. It has been carried by explorers and seafarers as a light weight food source.

Remember, however, that true whole wheat bread contains the oils from the germ and they can go rancid very quickly. Dried bread made from home ground flour won't have the long shelf life that commercial de-germinated products offer.

Making Fluffier Whole Wheat Bread

To make good bread is easy and simple. Just follow the directions in the Recipes above. It is difficult to truly fail, especially if you are hungry. Making really great bread requires a little more subtlety and practice, but not much.

If you have made any of the bread recipes described above, you have noticed that the bread is heavier and denser than commercial bread. Using whole wheat flour has this effect because it contains far more fiber (bran) than commercial flour and the gluten has not been bleached. It is for this reason that many bakers and cookbooks specify combinations of white or unbleached flour and whole wheat flour.

It must be pointed out that any preference for the fluffier commercial breads over the denser basic whole wheat breads is strictly cultural and is only a relative point of view.

You can still make fluffier breads by allowing them to rise to more than two times their original size. The yeast is more active if they have sugar to metabolize. The sugar can be obtained by adding cane sugar, honey, malt, molasses, or by using sprouted wheat in the recipe. The addition of milk and eggs tends to improve the texture and prevent the bread from becoming crumbly or developing bubbles and collapsing or deflating during baking.

Bread comes out moister if you use a little extra liquid when kneading it. For optimum results, the dough should be only slightly sticky in the center of the mass while the surface is non-sticky. You can make the surface of the mass non-sticky by dusting a bit of dry flour on it.

Longer kneading also tends to produce better lighter bread. Sticky dough gets less sticky if kneaded long enough.

The following recipe is made to be lighter, fluffier, spongier, and moister. It is also a high protein bread recipe.

High Protein Bread

Combine the following ingredients:

2 cups whole wheat flour
1/4 cup dry milk powder
1 egg
1/2 tsp salt
1 tbs yeast
2 tbs honey
3/4 cup water
1/4 cup Legume Protein Complement

Mix and knead this mixture into stiff dough. Add additional liquid or dry flour if needed. Allow this dough to rise in a warm place until it is about three times the original height. Bake this dough at about 350 degrees F (177 degrees C) for about 45 minutes or until done.

Whole Wheat Crackers

Recipe 1:

Combine the following ingredients:

4 cups freshly ground flour
1 tbs oil
1 tsp salt
water to make stiff dough

Mix the dry ingredients, then add water and mix thoroughly. When you have stiff dough, roll it thin, and cut it into small squares and perforate these with a fork. Bake these in a hot oven until crisp.

Recipe 2:

Combine the following ingredients:

4 cups freshly ground flour
1 tbs oil
1 tbs salt
1 tsp baking soda
1 egg
enough buttermilk to make a stiff paste

Mix the ingredients thoroughly into stiff dough and roll it thin. Cut the dough into small squares and perforate them with a fork. Bake these at high temperature until crisp.

Recipe 3:

In 1 cup of warm water dissolve 1 tbs of honey or sugar and one tbs of yeast and allow the mixture to set for ten minutes. This is the yeast mixture.

Mix the following ingredients together:

4 cups fresh flour
2/3 cups milk powder
2 tsp salt
1/3 cup oil

Add to this mixture the yeast mixture and an additional cup of warm water. Knead the dough, form it into a ball, and allow it to rise for 1 hour. Using a handful of dough at a time, roll it into sheets as thin as possible. Bake on an ungreased cookie sheet at 350 degrees F (177 degrees C) for about 6 minutes, then turn it over and bake it another 3 minutes. Crackers are light weight because most of the water content is baked out. They make an excellent emergency and trail food.

Improvised Primitive Bread making

Pancakes can be cooked on a clean flat rock heated by a campfire. Primitive ovens can be improvised using rock reflectors and a campfire. It is less effort to simply take a clean stick, wrap any version of bread dough around the end of the stick, and roast it over the hot coals just as you would hot-dogs and marshmallows until it is ready to eat.

This takes a little patience to get the "stick bread" thoroughly baked. It is delicious and smells divine, especially to hungry campers. Every time that I do this, the campfire gourmets wind up eating the stick bread half raw and grabbing for more.

Fresh clean sifted wood ashes will serve as a direct substitute for baking soda or baking powder if you have none. The use of wood ashes was common among American Indian tribes.

Caution! Use only WOOD ashes. DO NOT use ashes that contain residue from newspapers, boxes, plastic, or other items. Some of these manufactured materials contain toxic substances.

Backpackers should consider bread making on the trail more seriously. Dry flour has about the same weight and energy content as freeze dried food packages and costs considerably less. You can ferment your sourdough mixture in a quart sized large mouth plastic bottle that has a pop off spout. The pop off feature is important because it relieves the pressure from the bubbling expanding brew. Putting a fresh sourdough mixture in a tightly closed container, shaking it up by walking, getting it hot as the sun warms you and your pack up, and reducing atmospheric pressure by going up in altitude can create an explosion.

Pan Bread

The fastest method of making bread is in an iron skillet on the stovetop. Pancakes, biscuits, flat breads, cornbread, thin loaves, and traditional Native American fry breads are prepared this way. The bread dough can be leavened as with any of the yeast recipes described above. The dough made from sourdough and sprouted wheat methods also work very well. Any bread dough recipe can be used. The principles that are important, not the recipe.

Basic Principles of Pan Bread

Here are some of the principles that apply to making good pan bread:

- If you are using a yeast or sourdough recipe, give it a reasonable amount of time to rise.

- If you are using baking powder recipe, allow about ten minutes before cooking.

- Adjust the water content to get stiff non-sticky dough.

- Flatten the dough till it is no more than one quarter inch thick. This makes it cook quickly and evenly.

- Cook it in a cast iron skillet or Dutch oven.

Fry Bread

Here are some traditional Native American "fry bread" recipes.

Blackfoot Frybread Recipe

4 cups flour
1 tbs powdered milk
1 tbs baking powder
1 tsp salt
11/2 cups warm water
Oil for frying

Cherokee Frybread Recipe

1 cup flour
1/2 tsp salt
2 tsp baking powder
3/4 cup milk

Chickasaw Frybread Recipe

2 cups sifted flour
1/2 tsp salt
4 tsp baking powder
1 egg
1/2 cup warm milk

Creek Frybread Recipe

2 cups flour
1 cup buttermilk
1 tbs baking powder
1/4 tsp salt

You get the idea. Follow the basic principles and pretty much anything goes. You can:

- Use any kind of flour or meal or any mixture of flours. Corn, millet, rye, triticale, oat flour, etc. All work.

- You can add legume proteins to increase protein content. Heat processed soy flour, lupine flour, peanut powder, etc. all work. If used, they should be added in the ratio of 1unit of legume powder or flour to 3 units of grain flour.

- You can add any kind of nuts and any kind of dried fruits and berries to the dough.

- Fresh berries and fruits should be generally avoided because they contain a lot of water and can make the final product too gooey.

- You can add eggs, milk, buttermilk, yogurt, etc. or just use water.

- You can use yeast, sourdough starter or just baking powder to get the bread to rise.

- You can deep fry it in hot oil in the traditional Native American style or use the low fat approach and just bake it in the skillet.

- You can cook it fast in a hot skillet and brown both sides, or bake it slowly in a lower temperature skillet.

- You can top a large flat piece of fry bread with beans and cheese, etc. and eat it like a large tortilla.

- You can top a large flat piece of fry bread with pizza fixings and eat it like a pan pizza.

- The more you experiment, the more variety you have.

Making Noodles, Pasta and Dumplings

Pasta is usually made from durum wheat. For the best results with pasta, grind durum wheat for flour. If you don't have durum, you can use hard red wheat with satisfactory results. You can purchase pasta machines that extrude noodle filaments of various sizes and shapes. For storage, these noodles are hung on a rack and dried. Noodles can also be made by rolling the lump of dough thin with a rolling pin and cutting the noodles with a knife.

Making Pasta

Recipe 1:

Combine the following ingredients:

2 cups whole wheat flour
1/2 cup Legume Protein Complement
1 tsp salt (optional)
2 tsp baking powder (optional)
1 cup water to make stiff dough

Knead this dough for a few minutes then roll it out into a large thin pancake about 1/16 inch thick. Cut it into strips 1/4 to 1/2 inches wide. These noodles taste good and hold together well. They don't have the cohesiveness to make fine noodles the size of spaghetti, however.

Recipe 2:

1 1/4 cups whole wheat flour
1/4 cup Legume Protein Complement
2 eggs

Mix the dry ingredients, form a depression in the middle of the flour, and break the eggs into this depression. Beat the eggs with a fork and slowly mix in the flour until you have formed smooth dough. Knead this for about 10 minutes, roll it flat with a rolling pin, and cut it into noodles with a knife. Sprinkle a bit of flour onto your cutting board to help prevent sticking. Depending on the size of the eggs, type of flour, and humidity, you may need to add a very small amount of water or flour to the dough to get the right consistency.

Recipe 3:

Combine the following ingredients in a mixing bowl:

1 1/4 cups whole wheat flour
1 tsp salt
1/2 cup oil or butter
1/4 cup Legume Protein Complement
A little water to make stiff dough

Knead this for about 10 minutes, roll it flat with a rolling pin, and cut it into noodles with a knife.

Basic Noodles

Drop the fresh noodles into boiling salted water. Drop them in one at a time so they don't stick together. Boil for about ten minutes or until tender. Cooking time will be affected by their size and thickness.

Dumplings

A dumpling is really just a big fat noodle that is made fresh from scratch. There are many recipes for making dumplings. Here is a typical one:

2 eggs, beaten
3/4 cup milk (use water if you have no milk)
2 1/2 cups whole wheat flour
1/2 cup Legume Protein Complement
1 tbs baking powder, sifted in
1 tsp salt

Beat this mixture thoroughly and knead. Either form it into small balls or roll it flat and cut it into squares one to two inches square. Drop these into boiling water one at a time and cook them for about 20 minutes.

In addition to the traditional recipes, you can use virtually any bread recipe. Reduce the liquid content a little to make the dough very stiff, roll it thin and cut it into dumplings. Sourdough dumplings and yeast dumplings made in this manner are delicious.

Meat and Dumplings

Boil the chicken (or rabbit, beef, or whatever else you have, can find, or can catch) and remove the meat from the bones. Separate the meat out for another meal. Leave the liquid stock and some of the meat scraps as flavoring. Add salt to taste to the broth. Add chopped carrots, potatoes, onions, and green peas (and/or other available vegetables) and cook these ingredients for about 5 minutes. Drop fresh dumplings into the boiling meat and broth mixture and cook them for another 20 minutes.

Split Peas and Dumplings

Make a basic soup using split peas. If split peas are unavailable, use lentils or any other legume.

To two quarts of boiling water add one half cup of split peas and simmer till they are soft. Add two cups of chopped vegetables, a mixture of fresh or dried onions, carrots, green peas, celery, cabbage, nettles, or whatever else is available. Simmer for another two minutes and add soy sauce or miso to taste. Make one of the dumpling mixes and drop a half tsp at a time into the simmering soup. Cook another twenty minutes and serve.

Another Dumpling Recipe

Combine the following ingredients in a mixing bowl:

1 1/2 cups whole wheat flour
3 tsp baking powder
1/2 cup Legume Protein Complement
1 tsp salt
1 tsp honey
2 tbs oil
3/4 cup boiling water
1/4 tsp thyme
1/4 tsp nutmeg
1/4 tsp cloves
1/3 cup chopped parsley (or any other fresh herb)

Drop this batter into the simmering soup, stew, or salted water one teaspoonful a time.

Potato Dumplings

Combine the following ingredients in a mixing bowl:

1 cup cold mashed potatoes
1/2 cup whole wheat flour
1 egg
Salt and pepper to taste

Mix these ingredients into stiff dough and cut or tear out two inch square pieces. Drop these into a simmering soup or stew.

Making Gluten Meat Substitute

Wheat contains a protein called gluten. The gluten can be easily extracted and used as a high protein meat substitute. Don't forget that gluten will be low in some of the essential amino acids, especially Lysine. It, therefore, should be combined with legume proteins such as TVP, heat processed soy flour, peanut meal or peanut butter, cooked beans or sweet lupine flour. Alternately, the "wheat meat" made from gluten can be combined with beans in a meal. If this is done, the protein quality and quantity will provide an adequate substitute for meat protein.

It will still be lacking in certain vitamins and minerals normally found in animal foods and these will have to be provided from other sources. The flavor is another issue. This stuff doesn't taste like meat but will take on whatever flavor you cook it with. To achieve an approximately balanced protein combination, use gluten and TVP, soy flour, or sweet lupine flour in equal proportions.

Extracting gluten from wheat flour does require more work and preparation than using cooked whole wheat or whole wheat flour. Some people throw away the starch and water which contains most of the B vitamins. You can save the carbohydrates, bran, and B vitamins by using the cracker recipe below or by using the liquid slurry as a soup or stew stock.

If you are a serious cook, Gluten meat substitute can be composed into some truly delicious meals. Perhaps the change of pace will make it worth the extra effort required to process the wheat.

Quite frankly, the amount of time and effort this requires makes it impractical in a survival situation. Throwing away part of the wheat is also a waste of calories that are needed for survival. Make gluten meat substitute if it intrigues you or you are bored and don't have anything more important to worry about.

Extracting Gluten

Combine about 10 cups of fresh flour with just enough water to make stiff dough, about 3 to 4 cups. Knead this dough very thoroughly, for at least 15 minutes. Then knead and wash the dough ball gently in about 3 quarts of cold water. Pour off the creamy solution and repeat with fresh water. When the soft dough has become firm, the starch has been removed. The liquid residue from the washing process contains the bran, germ, starch, and most of the B vitamins from the wheat. You can use it as a soup stock as is or you can separate the sediment out and make crackers with it.

Ground Beef Substitute

Marinate the gluten pieces in soy sauce or meat broth then grind them up and combine them with equal parts of TVP. Use this mixture in place of hamburger in chili, soups, or casseroles. To make patties or meatballs, you will need to add eggs and/or a little oil and flour to get it to stick together. You may also wish to add sausage spices or other meat enhancing spice combinations to give it additional flavor. Use this for making 'hamburger patties' or as a substitute for ground beef in any recipe calling for it.

Wheat Beefsteaks

Mix 1 cup of TVP with 1 cup of raw gluten. Divide the two cups of protein mixture into a half dozen pieces and pound them into steakettes. Place the following ingredients into a pot:

3 cups water	1/4 cup soy sauce
1/2 tsp pepper	1 tbs. oil
1 tsp ground cumin	steakettes
1 tsp ground coriander	
1 tsp garlic powder	

You may fry the steakettes lightly on both sides or serve them as is. The broth can be served as a light soup.

Gluten Free Crackers

From the liquid left over from separating the gluten from the flour, a residue will settle to the bottom of the container. Pour off the liquid. The liquid contains most of the B vitamins so it should be reused as cooking water or soup stock.

Warm the residue but don't get it hot. Mix in a small amount of honey or malt and yeast. Stir this well and allow it to rise for 30 minutes. Pour this mixture onto well oiled cookie sheets and allow it to rise for another 30 minutes. Bake at 300 degrees F (150 degrees C) until the crackers are thoroughly dried out and crisp. These crackers resemble Scandinavian hard bread.

Cooking with Corn

Wheat, rye, spelt, kamut and triticale can be used pretty much interchangeably in the recipes and preparation methods described above. They do have different qualities and flavors but it is all good. Oats, barley and buckwheat are more challenging to store for long periods and offer different flavors and nutritional qualities.

Corn is a bit different. It is important because it is a high yielding grain, is easy to grow and handle by an individual without special equipment, and is relatively inexpensive to buy. There are many varieties of corn with different agricultural and culinary qualities.

Corn was a staple in Native American diets prior to European colonization. The North American natives processed corn into hominy by soaking it in lye (potassium hydroxide) that was obtained by leaching wood ashes. In Mexico, Central and South America, slaked lime (calcium hydroxide) was used instead. In either case the alkali treatment made the B vitamin Niacin biologically available. Individuals living on a diet based on alkali treated corn (the Native Americans) did not suffer from pellagra while those who consumed a diet based on untreated corn (the white colonists) did.

Pellagra is a nasty disease caused by Niacin deficiency. Pellagra is characterized by diarrhea, dermatitis and dementia along with aggressiveness, weakness, red skin lesions, insomnia, peripheral neuritis and high sensitivity to light. This is a deficiency condition rather than a toxic condition. Individuals who get niacin and the amino acid tryptophan from other sources do not have this problem.

Cornmeal made from alkali treated corn is called masa and is used in Mexican foods like tortillas and tamales. Most commercial cornmeal in North America is simply ground corn that has not been alkali treated. As long as one gets an abundance of B vitamins from other sources, this should not be a problem.

In contemporary times, wood ashes are no longer commonly available. Commercial food grade lye has become difficult to find because lye sale is restricted. Lye is an ingredient used in some illegal drug manufacture. Lime (calcium hydroxide) is preferred anyway because it adds a bit of calcium to the hominy. Lime is sold as pickling lime in canning supply outlets. An alternate method uses baking soda for the alkali agent. All three methods are described here for reference.

Lye Hominy

This method is described for information purposes only. In a pinch, one could improvise using wood ashes as the source of lye.

- Place 2 quarts of dry field corn in an enamel or stainless steel pan.

- Add 8 quarts of water and 2 ounces of food grade lye. Add the lye slowly. It releases heat when it mixes with water. If you were using wood ashes, you would mix water and ashes and filter the liquid, and then add the corn.

- Boil for 30 minutes, and then allow it to stand for 20 minutes.

- Rinse off lye with several hot water rinses.

- Follow with cold water rinses to cool for handling. It is very important to rinse the corn thoroughly.

- Work hominy with your hands or a wooden implement until the dark tips of the kernels are loosened from the rest of the kernel (about 5 minutes). Separate the tips from the corn by floating them off in water or by placing the corn in a coarse sieve and washing thoroughly.

- Add sufficient water to cover the hominy by about 1 inch. Boil 5 minutes and change the water. Repeat four times.

- Cook until the kernels are soft (30 to 45 minutes) and drain.

Baking Soda Hominy

- Use 2 Tablespoons of baking soda to 2 quarts of water for 1 quart of dry field corn. Add the baking soda to the water and bring it to a boil while stirring to dissolve the baking soda.

- Add the dry field or hominy corn, stirring continuously to prevent sticking. Boil vigorously for 30 minutes, stirring occasionally.

- Allow it to stand for 20 minutes. Rinse off the baking soda solution with several changes of hot water. Follow with cold water rinses to cool for handling. It is very important to rinse the corn thoroughly.

- Work the hominy with your hands or a wooden implement until the dark tips of kernels are loosened from the rest of the kernel (about 5 minutes). Separate the tips from the corn by floating them off in water or by placing the corn in a coarse sieve and washing thoroughly.

- Cook until the kernels are soft (30 to 45 minutes) and drain.

Lime Hominy

- Mix 4 quart of water and 5 tablespoons of slaked lime (pickling lime or calcium hydroxide). Use a non-reactive pot like stainless steel – not aluminum or iron. Heat and stir this mixture until all of the lime is dissolved.

- Add 3 pounds (2 quarts) of corn, bring to a boil and simmer and soak. The simmering and soaking time varies depending on the intended application.

- For Hominy, boil for 15 minutes and let it soak for 15 minutes. For tortillas, bring the mixture to a boil then remove it from the heat and let it soak overnight. For tamale dough, boil it for 15 minutes, and then let it soak for 1 1/2 hours.

- Drain the corn in a large colander and rinse it with several changes of water. Then use your fingers or a wooden tool to rub the corn, removing all traces of lime. If you are making hominy, it will be necessary to remove the hulls at this time.

- Put the hulled corn into a large bowl and cover with lukewarm water. Allow it to soak for 5-10 minutes while moving the corn around with a wooden paddle or tool. Drain the finished corn through a colander.

- Grind the corn if you are making tamales or tortillas. Since this is a soft wet product, a regular grain grinder may not work. Stone burs are, of course, not appropriate. A meat grinder with the fine plates and blades may suffice. In a standard kitchen under normal conditions, a food processor may work.

Caution Warning!!!

Lye and lime are strong alkalis and are dangerous. Heat is generated when water and the alkali are mixed. To avoid problems always add the lye or lime very slowly while stirring thoroughly.

Always wear eye protection. If you accidently get some in an eye, wash it thoroughly with cool water immediately then get medical attention.

Lye and lime can cause chemical burns if you get some on your skin. Putting your hands in lye water can cause "drying" as the lye reacts with the oils in your skin. Always wear gloves when handling lye or lye water.

Corn Bread

Corn bread is an extremely versatile dish. It can form the foundation for many combination "meal in one" dishes. Cornbread is probably the simplest bread to make — no kneading, no rising, no expensive ingredients, quick baking and it's nearly impossible to screw up.

Making Cornbread

Recipe 1

1 1/2 to 2 cup corn meal
boiling hot water
pinch of salt (may use more or less depending on taste)

Pour only enough hot water in corn meal to mix all ingredients well. It should not be too watery or the meal will not hold together. Form in small round patties. Deep fry for about 6 to 8 minutes in a skillet, on each side, or until golden brown and crisp.

Recipe 2

2 cup fresh ground corn meal
1 tsp salt
1 1/2 cup cold water (or enough to make a soft mixture that can be spooned like pancake batter)
4 tbs olive, coconut or peanut oil or butter

Mix the corn meal, salt and water. Preheat the oven to 475 degrees F (245 degrees C) and heat the oil in a 9 inch round iron skillet in the hot oven. Carefully spread this mixture evenly in the hot skillet. Bake this for about 15 minutes or until it is golden brown. Alternately, add small amounts to a hot skillet to about the size and thickness of a pancake. Flip it over when bubbles begin to appear in the middle.

Recipe 3

2 cup whole grain freshly ground Corn Meal
2 tsp baking powder
1 tsp soda
1 tsp salt
1 egg
2 tbs oil – olive, coconut or butter
1 3/4 cup buttermilk or yogurt

Put the oil in a cast iron skillet. Mix the ingredients in a bowl until they are blended and moist. Pour the batter into the cast iron skillet. Bake the mix at 400 degrees F (200 degrees C) until done (about 30 minutes).

Many cornbread recipes call for one half wheat flour and one half cornmeal. You can rise the wheat and corn mixture with yeast or sourdough starter. You can omit the egg or use two instead of one. You can also use the equivalent amount of powdered eggs. You can omit the oil or use more (you need some to oil the skillet). Many recipes call for white sugar, but white sugar does not constitute food in my book. Also, cornbread made with a lot of sugar doesn't taste like "real" cornbread. You can add honey, but I enjoy it more when smeared on the finished product. You can substitute sweet milk, evaporated milk or milk powder or omit it completely. The lactic acid in buttermilk and yogurt do react with the baking powder and soda to texture the cornbread, however. An old pioneer trick was to add a small amount of apple cider vinegar to the mix to help it rise. When you lack an ingredient, just omit it or substitute something that you do have. Corn bread is very adaptable and will tolerate a lot of modification.

You can add to the basic cornbread mix:

- Finely chopped and sauteed greens – collard greens, kale, mustard greens or wildcrafted greens.
- Shredded Cheese.
- Jalapeno peppers or other peppers.
- Dried tomatoes.
- Onions.
- Beans.
- Meat, fish or chicken.
- Bean sprouts.
- Boiled or roasted peanuts.
- Peanut butter.
- And other stuff.

With the added ingredients complementing the cornbread, you can make a complete meal.

Recipe 4

1 cup corn meal
1/2 cup whole wheat flour
3 tsp baking powder
1 tsp salt
1 cup grated extra sharp cheddar cheese
8 oz sour cream
1/4 cup oil - olive, coconut or peanut or butter
1 medium onion (chopped)
1 10 oz. can whole kernel corn (with liquid)
2 eggs
1 jalapeno pepper, sliced (as many as you dare)

Place a seasoned iron skillet with 1 tbs of oil in the oven and heat it to 350 degrees F (177 degrees C). Mix all of the dry ingredients together, add the other ingredients (saving a little cheese) and mix well with a spoon. Pour this mix into the hot skillet, sprinkle cheese on top and bake until it is light brown (25-30 minutes).

Recipe 5

2 tbs oil
1 3/4 cup fresh ground whole wheat flour
1 cup fresh ground cornmeal
1 cup oatmeal or rolled oats
2 tsp baking powder
2 tsp salt
1 1/2 tsp baking soda
2 cup buttermilk
2 eggs
1/4 cup olive, coconut or peanut oil or butter
1/3 cup sliced green onions

Place the oil in a 10-inch iron skillet and place the skillet in a preheated 375 degrees F (190 degree C) oven. Combine the flour, cornmeal, oats, baking powder, salt and soda. Stir in the buttermilk, eggs, oil and green onions. Pour this into a hot prepared skillet and bake at 375 degrees F (190 degree C) for 30 to 35 minutes.

Recipe 6

2 cup fresh ground whole wheat flour
2 cup fresh ground cornmeal
1 cup dry milk powder
2 tbs baking powder
1 tsp salt
1/2 tsp baking soda
2 2/3 cup water
1/2 cup butter, coconut oil, olive oil or peanut oil
2 eggs, beaten
1 tbs lemon juice (or apple cider vinegar)

Combine the flour, cornmeal, milk powder, baking powder, salt and baking soda. Add water, butter, eggs and lemon juice. Then stir until the dry ingredients are moistened. Spoon this into a muffin pan. Bake at 425 degrees F (220 degrees C) for 12-15 minutes.

Recipe 7

1 cup hominy
1 tbs. butter, coconut or olive oil, melted
2 eggs, beaten
1 cup milk
1/2 cup fresh ground cornmeal
1/2 tsp salt
1 tsp baking powder

Combine the hominy, oil, eggs, and milk. Add the cornmeal, salt and baking powder. Let it stand for 5 minutes. Pour this mixture into a large well oiled pan and bake it at 425 degrees F (220 degrees C) for 35 minutes or until it is a deep golden brown.

Recipe 8

1 cup sourdough starter
1 1/2 cup evaporated milk
1 1/2 cup yellow corn meal
2 whole eggs, beaten
1/4 cup butter, coconut or olive oil
1/2 tsp salt
1/2 tsp soda

Mix the starter, milk, corn meal, and eggs and stir thoroughly in a large bowl. Stir in the melted butter, salt, and soda. Place this in a 10 inch oiled frying pan and bake it at 450 degrees F (230 degrees C) for 20 minutes or until it tests done. (Stick a fork in the middle. When it comes out without dough clinging, it is done.)

Recipe 9

1 cup freshly ground corn meal
1 tbs. baking powder
1 cup shredded sharp cheddar
2 eggs
1/2 cup coconut, olive or peanut oil or butter
1 cup sour cream
8 oz corn; cream style, 1 can
4 oz green chile peppers; chopped

Preheat the oven to 400 degrees F (200 degrees C). Preheat and oil an iron skillet. In a large bowl, combine the cornmeal, baking powder and cheese. In a bowl, beat the eggs, oil, sour cream, corn and chilies together. Add to the cornmeal mixture. Stir until just moistened and then spoon the batter into the prepared pan. Bake for 40 to 50 minutes in the preheated oven until a wooden pick inserted in the center comes out clean. Cool on a rack for 10 minutes then invert over a serving plate.

Recipe 10

1 lb hamburger
1 can tomato sauce or equivalent
1 can whole kernel corn
2 tbs chili powder
1 large onion chopped
1 green pepper chopped
2 cup water
2 cup whole grain freshly ground Corn Meal
2 tsp baking powder
1 tsp soda
1 tsp salt

Preheat the oven to 400 degrees F (200 degrees C). Brown the hamburger and onion. Drain and add tomato sauce, water, corn, chili powder, and salt. Place the mixture in a large iron skillet. Pour the cornmeal, baking soda and baking powder mixture over the hamburger mixture and bake at 400 degrees F (200 degrees C) for 30 or 40 minutes.

Tempeh

Tempeh is an Indonesian dish made by a natural culturing and controlled fermentation process that binds soybeans into a cake form. Tempeh's fermentation process and its retention of the whole bean give it a higher content of protein, fiber, and vitamins. The fermentation process destroys the anti-nutritional and gas producing properties of the soybeans. This fermentation process converts soybeans into food.

It is important to note that the tempeh fermentation process is not restricted to soybeans. You can also use it on other beans, legumes and grains or any combination. The important thing to remember is that this fermentation agent is a fungus and it requires abundant oxygen. If any part of the fermenting mixture is lacking in oxygen exposure, it may spoil. This favors medium to large seeded grains and legumes to some degree.

How to make Tempeh

- Soak and dehull 1 lb (1/2 kg) of whole soybeans. Soak the beans for 8 - 14 hours in water and then remove the hulls by hand. In doing so, the beans are split into two halves and the seed coats can be discarded.

- Place the soybeans in a cooking pot and add just enough water to cover the beans. Add 1-2 tbs. of vinegar, bring the beans to the boiling point and simmer for 20 minutes. Drain and remove the cooked beans onto towels to drain off the excess water and to cool the beans, which are now swollen and soft. It's important that the beans become very dry on their surface; otherwise undesirable bacteria can grow and create off-flavors.

- Put the cool and dry beans in a clean container and sprinkle them with 1 teaspoon of tempeh starter and mix thoroughly. The exact amount of tempeh starter required is given on the package of tempeh starter.

- Take 2 plastic bags about 18x28 cm (7x12 inches) and perforate them with holes at a distance of about 1 cm (1/2 inch) by a sharp knife. Divide the soya beans in the two bags and seal them. Press them flat, making sure that the total thickness of the beans is not more than 3 cm. Place the packed beans in an incubator at 30°C (86°F) or at a warm place for about 24-48 hours or until the container is filled completely with white mycelium and the entire contents can be lifted out as a whole piece. A simple incubator can be made with putting a light bulb or heating pad in an ice chest. Remember that the tempeh will also produce some heat on its own.

The fresh tempeh will feel warm and will have a pleasant mushroom flavor. The finished tempeh can be stored in the refrigerator for 7 days or in the freezer for a few months.

Making Tempeh Starter

If you want to sustain tempeh production, you will want to make and save your own starter. For this, you need to start with a known starter culture.

Make tempeh as usual, but for one batch use a gallon size plastic bag and pat the mixture out very thin. After mycelium covers the tempeh and black spots form on holes in the bag, remove the tempeh from the bag and place it on a dry cloth in the same warm place where it grew. Let the surface become mottled or blackish with spores. Next crumble this material on a plate and let it air dry for a day. Then mix this material with equal parts of flour and dry it for another day. Then grind it to powder in a burr type grain mill or equivalent. Use about 1 Teaspoon per batch--as usual, but you may need to adjust up depending on how many spores you let grow before drying and grinding.

Tempeh can be cooked and made into a variety of dishes and can be, in general, used as a meat substitute.

Fried Tempeh

1/2 lb (500 grams) fresh tempeh
1 clove garlic, peeled and crushed
4 tbs oil
1/4 tsp salt

Cut the tempeh in thin slices. Put the oil and garlic in a skillet and sauté the tempeh slices on both sides until it is crispy and golden brown. Sprinkle it with the salt. This can be eaten as a snack, used as an ingredient in other recipes or eaten on a sandwich. You can substitute tempeh for ground beef in any recipe calling for meat or ground beef.

Tangy Tempeh with Peanut Sauce

For the marinade, mix the following:

2 tbs coconut or peanut oil
4 tbs soy sauce
2 tbs apple cider vinegar
1/3 cup wine
1 clove garlic, minced

Put 1/2 pound (250 g) tempeh, cut in small cubes, into a wide sauté pan, pour the marinade over the tempeh and simmer over low heat for 15 minutes. Uncover the tempeh and cook it until the tempeh is nearly dry. To make the peanut sauce mix the following ingredients:

1 cup peanut butter
2 tbs honey
2 tbs soy sauce
2 tbs apple cider vinegar
1 tsp fresh gingerroot, minced
2 cloves garlic, crushed
Jalapeno, Chili or other pepper sauce to taste
1/2 cup hot water

Serve over rice, cooked wheat berries, cooked oat groats, or cooked barley and top with peanut sauce.

Tempeh Chili

Put 1/2 pound (250 g) diced tempeh with one cup (200 ml) water in a large frying pan, add the soy sauce and simmer for 15 minutes at high heat until most of the water is absorbed. Drain and mash the tempeh with a fork to obtain small chunks. Add 2 tablespoons of coconut oil and sauté the tempeh for 10 minutes until it is slightly crisp. In a separate iron skillet, add the following:

1 tbs coconut oil
1 large onion, chopped
1 green or red bell pepper, chopped
Jalapeno or chili peppers (to taste), chopped
1 large carrot, cut in small cubes (optional)

Sautee lightly. Add the following:

2 clove garlic, crushed
2 tbs chili powder
1 tsp cumin powder
1 tsp dried oregano
the fried tempeh
2 cups (400 ml) of tomato sauce
1 can beans (pinto, black or kidney)
4 medium tomatoes, diced
2 tablespoon apple cider vinegar

Serve this tempeh chili with cornbread.

Sources of Tempeh Starter

GEM Cultures, Inc.
P.O. Box 39426
Lakewood, WA 98496
(253)588-2922
http://gemcultures.com

Indonesian Tempeh Online Store
Rockville, MD 20853, USA

(301)806-8118
http://tempehstarter.com

Cast Iron Cooking and Baking

Cast iron cookware was the mainstay of pioneer times, largely because that was all that was available. It persists in modern times where more choices in stainless steel, ceramics, etc. are available. The reason that it is still preferred by many is that cast iron distributes heat evenly across its surface and minimizes the tendency to scorch and burn food. Thus it is preferred for frying and baking. Cast iron utensils have this property because iron is only a fair conductor of heat and the pans are relatively thick.

The disadvantages of cast iron are that if the pots, pans, griddles, and Dutch ovens are not properly seasoned, the food will stick and the utensils will rust. Cast iron utensils that are improperly seasoned and improperly used can add too much iron to food. Too much iron can be unhealthy.

To avoid this problem:

- Avoid cooking liquid foods or boiling water in cast iron pots.

- Avoid cooking acid foods (like tomatoes and fruits) in cast iron.

- Keep the iron pots and pans properly seasoned at all times.

- Always empty, clean, dry and oil the iron utensils immediately after using them.

- Never use soap on cast iron.

- Never put cast iron utensils in a dish washer.

Cleaning Cast Iron

Cleaning cast iron should be done in a way that does not damage the seasoning or finish. The seasoned surface consists of carbon and oils that have filled in the pores of the iron giving it a smooth non-stick surface.

For pans that have already been seasoned, clean them by washing them with water only (no soap). Use only a soft cloth, brush or sponge. Rinse thoroughly, and dry immediately. Never soak the pans, especially in soapy water. Never put them into a dish washer. Dry immediately after washing. Place the pan over the burner for a couple of minutes and make certain that it is bone dry. Apply a small amount of oil to the surface. Coconut oil is a good choice because it is saturated oil and resists rancidity and withstands heating. Animal fat also works well.

Special cleaning attention needs to be given to new cast iron utensils. Some new cast iron comes with a protective coating. This can be a seasoning that is good to cook on or an "unidentified" protective material to protect the utensil from rust. If it is coated with an "unidentified" material, it is probably best to remove it and season the pan properly.

One approach to removing this material is to heat the utensil and burn the coating off. This is a bit risky because cast iron that is poorly made may warp or crack when it gets too hot or is heated unevenly or too fast. I have done this many times and never cracked a utensil. Others report that they have cracked their utensils this way. My approach has been to put the utensil in an open fire or inside a wood stove and get it red hot. A safer approach is to place it in your oven and set the oven to "self clean" for a couple of hours. This will generate a temperature of around 550 degrees F (290 degrees C).

Seasoning Cast Iron

If your old or new cast iron pans get light rust spots, scour the rusty areas with steel wool, until all traces of rust are gone. You can also scour the surface with salt and oil using a cloth or paper towel. Salt serves as a mild abrasive that will clean the surface without damaging it. Rinse, dry, and repeat the seasoning process.

To season a cast iron utensil, clean it thoroughly, apply a coating of oil and subject it to high heat. The oil chosen should be saturated oil like coconut oil or animal fat.

If too much oil or shortening is applied to a pan in the seasoning process, it will pool and gum up when the pan is heated. In this case, the goo can be smoothed out by gently heating the pan at low heat and rubbing with a cloth or paper towel and fresh oil.

One seasoning approach is to wipe the pan with oil and place it in a 350 degree F (180 degree C) oven for one to two hours. Then remove the pan and let it cool. Then wipe it with fresh oil and heat it again. Repeat this for three to six cycles. The repeated heating and cooling opens and closes the pores in the iron embedding an oily film in the surface. The heat also polymerizes the oil converting it into a more durable coating.

Another approach is to wipe the pan with oil, place it onto a burner, heat it to the smoking point, remove it and let it cool. Wipe the cooled pan with fresh oil and repeat the cycle for three to six times.

Cooking Pan Bread in Cast Iron

To cook pan bread in cast iron, lightly oil the skillet, heat it till a drop of water on the surface sizzles and place the flat piece of bread dough in the skillet. Place a lid on the skillet and reduce the heat to very low. An iron lid works best because it picks up heat from the pan and helps cook the top side of the bread. It is done when it is spongy and a knife or fork inserted into the bread does not remove any sticky dough.

Conversions for Baking and Cooking

1 Tablespoon =3 Teaspoons
2 Tablespoons =1 Ounce
4 Tablespoons =1/4 Cup
8 Tablespoons =1/2 Cup
12 Tablespoons =3/4 Cup
16 Tablespoons =1 Cup = 8 Fluid Ounces
2 Cups =1 Pint = 16 Fluid Ounces
2 Pints =1 Quart = 32 Fluid Ounces
2 Quarts =1/2 Gallon = 64 Fluid Ounces
4 Quarts =1 Gallon = 128 Fluid Ounces1 Cup All-Purpose
Flour =5 Ounces
1 Cup Cake Flour =4 Ounces
1 Cup Whole Wheat Flour =5 1/2 Ounces
1 Cup Granulated (White) Sugar =7 Ounces
1 Cup Packed Brown Sugar=7 Ounces
1 Cup Confectioners' Sugar =4 Ounces
1 Cup Cocoa Powder =3 Ounces
Butter 1/2 Stick or 1/4 Cup =4 Tablespoons of 2 Ounces
Butter 1 Stick or 1/2 Cup =8 Tablespoons or 4 Ounces
Butter 2 Sticks or 1 Cup =16 Tablespoons or 8 Ounces

1 ounce=30 milliliters
1 pint=0.47 liters
1 quart=.95 liters
1 gallon=3.8 liters
1 liter=1.06 quarts
1 liter=2.1 pints
1 kilogram=2.2 pounds
1 pound=0.45 kilograms
1 ounce=28.35 grams
1 gram=.04 ounces

Essential Tools and Supplies

Your basic collection of working tools should include the following:

(1) A good grain mill. Make certain that you have at least one that can be operated manually. Spend the extra money and buy a high quality machine.

(2) Two or three one gallon sized jars for sprouting wheat and sprouting trays for alfalfa and mung bean sprouts.

(3) An ice chest for keeping the sprouting containers warm.

(4) A flour sifter, rolling pin, measuring cups & spoons, mixing bowls, and other kitchen supplies.

(5) Two one quart wide mouth containers with pop off lids for sourdough starter.

(6) A tool for grinding wheat sprouts. This must be a metal burr type mill that disassembles and cleans easily or a small meat grinder with the same features.

(7)   Hand cranked wheat grass juicer.

(8) A hand cranked roller mill. These are useful for making rolled oats or wheat.

(9) At least one good cast iron skillet with a lid. Preferably two of different sizes. Dutch ovens are ideal for cooking on an open fire.

(10) A stainless steel pressure cooker.

How Much Wheat, Grains and Legumes Should You Store?

How much should you store? Wheat (and most other grains) contains about 1500 calories per pound. The average American consumes over 3000 calories per day. The number of calories that you actually need will vary with your body size, climate, season and physical activity level. If you store one pound of wheat per person per day for a two year supply, you will store 730 pounds of wheat per family member. If one is physically active and under stress, 1500 calories per day won't be enough. Other grains, legumes, fats and oils, and animal proteins are needed to make up the balance.

While wheat is a proven staple for both food qualities and long term storage, variety should be a part of planning. A portion of your grain stores should be committed to a mixture of other grains. Try them and store what you like. Store legumes for protein and to complement the protein in the grains. Store 1 pound of legumes to 3 pounds of grains.

For each person store the following supplied for each year of intended food insurance.

300 pounds wheat
100 pounds of legumes, beans and TVP
100 pounds of other grains (corn, millet, oats, buckwheat, rice, pasta, flour, etc.)
100 pounds of dried and canned fruits and Vegetables
70 pounds of dried milk
20 pounds of dried eggs
100 pounds of canned or freeze dried meats
25 pounds of honey
5 pounds of salt
15 pounds (2 gal.) oils (coconut and olive preferred)
2 pounds of baking powder, 2 pounds of baking soda
Bakers yeast, sourdough starter, tempeh starter
Multiple vitamin and multiple mineral supplements
Additional vitamin C

Resources

With the advent of the Internet, most of the resources that you need can be readily found with your favorite search engine. Here are a few suppliers to get you started.

Sources of Grain Mills

The Country Living Grain Mill

The Country Living Grain Mill
14727 56th Ave. N.W.
Stanwood, WA   98292
(360) 652-0671
http://www.countrylivinggrainmills.com/
countrylivinggrainmills@verizon.net

The country living mill is a high quality unit with ball bearings. It is set up to operate with a hand crank but has a large pulley which can be readily used with a motor or bicycle. It has metal burrs which produce very satisfactory flour in one grinding. An electric motor kit is available for these mills. This mill comes with a twenty year warranty, but you're not likely to ever need to use it. They offer an optional auger for beans and larger grains.

The Diamant Mill

The Diamant mills are manufactured in Denmark. They offer stone burrs and three different sets of metal burrs. It is a very heavy duty mill with ball bearings and a large pulley with a hand crank. It is readily adapted to motors or bicycles. Diamant Mills can be purchased from numerous retailers including:

Lehman's®
289 Kurzen Road North
Dalton, Ohio 44618
http://www.lehmans.com
info@lehmans.com
1-877-438-5346

The C.S. Bell Company

C.S. Bell Company
Box 291
170 West Davis St
Tiffin, Ohio   44883
419-448-0791
888-958-6381
http://www.csbellco.com/grinding-grist-mills.asp
sales@csbellco.com

This company makes a variety of mills designed for farm, ranch, and industrial uses. Their two smaller mills, the No. 2 and the Model 60 are suitable for home use. The No. 2 is a rugged hand cranked model with metal burrs and the Model 60 is a larger unit equipped with a pulley for motor drive. It has three different sets of metal burrs for different degrees of coarseness in the grind. It also has an optional hand crank. These mills are used to grind bones and hull sunflower seeds as well as grind flour. The No. 2 mill produces flour that requires sifting and a second grind to achieve bread making quality.

The Meadows Mill

Meadows Mills Company
1352 West D Street
PO Box 1288
North Wilkesboro, North Carolina   28659
336-838-2282
800-626-2282
http://www.meadowsmills.com/sbm8.htm
meadowsmills@charter.net

This company makes a variety of mills for farm, ranch, and timber operations. Their smallest grist mill is an 8 inch stone burr mill. It is unique in that it uses natural granite for the stones. The mill comes with a belt driven pulley on the shaft. Any adaptation to hand use would have to be done by the owner. This appears to be a quality, rugged, industrial grade unit that would be suited to a small bakery. It will grind 50 pounds per hour of wheat or 100 pounds per hour of corn.

Retsel Mills

Retsel Corporation
1567 Hwy 30
McCammon, Idaho   83250
208-254-3737
http://www.retsel.com/
service@retsel.com

This company makes a hand mill called the Little Ark and an electric model called the Mil-Rite. Both units are offered with both stone and metal burrs. The electric units come with removable hand cranks for use during power failures. They also offer the electric model without a motor. A user can then add a DC motor, gasoline motor, or bicycle drive. You can also use it as a hand mill. This mill is designed to turn at 60 rpm, a speed appropriate for hand operation. All electric Retsel mills have a 10 year manufacturer's warranty. All manual Retsel mills carry an unconditional lifetime warranty.

The Golden Grain Grinder

Kuest Enterprises
Box 110
Filer, Idaho   83328
208-326-4084
http://www.goldengraingrinder.com/
goldengrinder@hotmail.com

This company manufactures a high quality, high volume, electric mill that is housed in an attractive wooden cabinet. It has stainless steel burrs that can handle oily or dry grains, stone burrs, and a detachable handle for manual operation.

You can attach a Blackburn Trakstand to your bicycle, remove the fan from the trakstand and replace it with a pulley, attach a belt, and drive your grain mill with it. Check your nearest bicycle shop for the Blackburn Trakstand.

General Suppliers

The Survival Center
PO Box 234
McKenna, WA   98558
1-360-458-6778
http://survivalcenter.com
info@survivalcenter.com

    The Survival Center sells a wide variety of survival equipment, supplies, and books.

_____

Walton Feeds
Box 307
Montpelier, ID   83254
800-847-0465
208-847-0465
http://waltonfeed.com/
waltonfeed@waltonfeed.com

    This company sells bulk grains, bulk freeze dried foods, and other essential supplies for food storage.

_____

Wheat Montana Farms & Bakery

10778 Highway 287
Three Forks, MT 59752
1-800-535-2798
www.wheatmontana.com

    Wheat Montana sells their own variety of wheat specially selected for bread making, along with other grains, beans, and cereal. Their wheat is very high in protein (18%). Their website indicates that many walmart supercenters are now carrying their wheat in 25 pound bags.

_____

Bob's Red Mill
13521 SE Pheasant Court
Milwaukie, Oregon 97222
(800) 349-2173
(503) 654-3215
(800) 553-2258
http://www.bobsredmill.com

C.F. Resources
P.O. Box 405, Kit Carson, CO 80825
(719) 962-3228
http://cfamilyresources.com

Healthy Harvest
2903 NE 109th Avenue
Suite H
Vancouver, WA 98682
(360) 891-4408
(888) 311-8940
customerservice@healthyharvest.com
http://www.healthyharvest.com

Emergency Essentials, Inc.
653 North 1500 West
Orem, Utah 84057
1-800-999-1863
sales@beprepared.com
http://beprepared.com/

FrontierSurvival.com
5765 Hwy 64
Farmington, NM 87410
United States
505-947-2200
http://www.frontiersurvival.com

Grandma's Country...
386 West 9400 South,
Sandy, Utah 84070
801-748-0808
800-216-6466
http://www.grandmascountryfoods.com/

Honeyville Food Products, Inc.
11600 Dayton Drive
Rancho Cucamonga, CA 91730
Phone: (909) 980-9500 FAX: (909) 980-6503
http://honeyvillegrain.com

Life Sprouts
P.O. Box 150
Hyrum, UT 84319
(435)245-3891
To Order: (800)241-1516
Email: sales@lifesprouts.com
http://lifesprouts.com

SPROUTPEOPLE®
170 Mendell St.
San Francisco, CA 94124
877/777-6887
http://sproutpeople.com/

This is an outstanding source for sprouting information,
sprouting supplies and sproutable seeds and grains.

Major Surplus & Survival
435 W. Alondra
Gardena, CA, 90248
Sales: Sales@MajorSurplus.com
http://majorsurplusandsurvival.com/

Nitro-Pak Preparedness Center, Inc.
375 W. 910 S.
Heber City, UT 84032
Order Toll Free: 1.800.866.4876
http://www.nitro-pak.com

Ready Made Resources
Customer Service and Ordering: 423-253-6789
Mailing Address: 239 Cagle Road
Tellico Plains, TN 37385
http://readymaderesources.com

Best Prices Storable Foods
P.O. Box 3182
Quinlan, Texas 75474
(903) 356-6443 (9a-6p)
http://www.internet-grocer.net

(Sourdough Starter)
Oregon Trail Sourdough
P. O. Box 321
Jefferson, MD 21755 USA
http://carlsfriends.net/source.html

Sourdoughs International
PO Box 670
Cascade, Idaho   83611
208-382-4828
http://sourdo.com/culture.htm

This is an excellent source for some great sourdough starters.

Lodge Cast Iron
http://www.lodgemfg.com/site-map.asp

GEM Cultures, Inc.
P.O. Box 39426
Lakewood, WA 98496
(253)588-2922
http://gemcultures.com/

This is a good source for tempeh starter as well as
sourdough, soy cultures, kombuchu culture, and dairy
cultures.

_____

Indonesian Tempeh Online Store.
Rockville, MD 20853, USA
Phone: (301)806-8118
http://tempehstarter.com/index.htm

This is a good source of a variety of tempeh starters and
information on making tempeh.

_____

http://offgridsurvival.com/survivalwebsites/

This is a link to a list of survival and sustainable living blogs.

Bibliography

How to Survive with Sprouting, Bruford Scott Reynolds, Hawkes Publishing, Inc., 1973

The Sprouting Book, Ann Wigmore, Avery Publishing Group, Inc., 1986

The Complete Sprouting Book, Per and Gita Sellman, Turnstone Press Limited, 1981

The Beansprout Book, Gay Courter, Simon and Schuster, 1973

SPROUTS To Grow and Eat, Esther Munroe, The Stephen Greene Press, 1974

Beginner's Guide to Family Preparedness, Rosalie Mason, Horizon Publishers, 1977

The Sprouter's Cookbook, Marjorie Blanchard, Garden Way Publishing, 1975

Diet for a Small Planet, Frances Moore Lappe, Ballentine, 1971

WHOLE GRAINS Grow, Harvest & Cook Your Own, Sara Pitzer, Garden Way Publishing, 1981

Whole Grain Baking, Diana Scesny Greene, The Crossing Press, 1984

How to Make all the Meat You Eat Out of Wheat, Nina & Michael Shandler, Rawson, Wade Publishers, Inc., 1980

The Dumpling Cookbook, Maria Polushkin, Workman Publishing Company, 1977

Professional Sourdough Cooking and Recipes, George Leonard Herter, Berthe E. Herter, 1975

<u>Home Food Systems</u>, Robert B. Yepsen, Jr. Ed., Rodale Press, 1981

<u>Making BREADS with Home-grown YEASTS & Home-grown Grains</u>, Phylis Hobson, Garden Way Press, 1974

<u>Alaska Sourdough</u>, Ruth Allman, Alaska Northwest Books, 1976

<u>Sprout Garden: Indoor Grower's Guide to Gourmet Sprouts</u>, Mark Braumstein, Book Publishing Company, 1999

<u>Sproutman's Kitchen Garden Cookbook</u>, Steve Myerowitz, The Sprout House, 1994

<u>World Sourdoughs from Antiquity</u>, Ed Wood, Ten Speed Press, 1999

<u>The Pulse Test: The Secret of Building Your Basic Health</u> by Arthur F. Coca, M.D., St. Martin's Press, 1996

Breinigsville, PA USA
24 February 2011
256214BV00004B/15/P